Getting to the Truth

A practical, scientific approach to behaviour analysis for professionals

C A Lansley

Printed in the United Kingdom.

First Published, January 2017

ISBN 978-1-5272-0634-2

Published by
Emotional Intelligence Academy Ltd
PO BOX 480, Sevenoaks, TN13 9JY, UK.
www.eiagroup.com
service@eiagroup.com

Includes Resources/Videos to support learning here:

www.gettingtothetruth.com

Contents

Table of Figures

Endorsements

"Preventing and countering terrorism is a matter of focus, analytic thinking, critical decision making and timely response. Behaviour Analysis is brought to the table through this book; an operational tool centred on SCAnR, to help investigators and operators be decisive in a split second based on this science-based skills and development model. We didn't get to the lightbulb by improving candles. This is a huge step away from the myths in Behaviour Analysis and shines the light on the truth."

('Scott' - Senior Counter Terrorism/Intelligence Professional)

"This book is designed to be a practical tool in high stakes scenarios. The topic of communications in high stakes medical settings have until now been largely overlooked. In my field of Emergency Medicine, there has been no equivalent work for assessing truthfulness as it relates to medical diagnosis and treatment. This book relates directly to the work I do treating patients in the acute setting and gives the reader tools to apply to difficult interactions in a rigorous yet compassionate manner. Cliff has achieved in making SCAnR applicable across disciplines, and I can no longer imagine practicing medicine without knowing how to assess my patients' words and behaviours across the six channels presented here."

(Dr. Timur Kouliev MD MBA FACEP EMDM)

"There is much debate, surrounding getting to the truth versus discerning lies. In this book, Cliff seeks to provide a useful "how to", whilst nonetheless nodding to some of these difficulties. His (i) research-based approach, (ii) provision of exercises, and (iii) inclusion of follow-up suggestions (of where the interested reader might find out more) all help to ensure that this book is a must read for those whose role (or life) equates to determining truth."

(Dawn Archer PhD – Professor of Pragmatics and Corpus Linguistics, Manchester Metropolitan University)

Cliff's book is excellent and clear. It gets to the important, practical aspects of detecting truth based on the scientific research and not the prevalent fads and fiction. This book is very useful for coaches, not because we are looking for client lies, but because noticing any incongruence and uncertainty will help us ask the best questions with attention and empathy.

(Joseph O'Connor, Executive coach and co-founder International Coaching Community)

"If you are interested in people and how we all react under pressure; you will find no clearer guide than this. Cliff's expertise helped my two documentaries attract record audiences for the Discovery TV channel, and a huge response in the wider media. Millions of viewers were fascinated to learn how to recognise tell-tale signs that reveal the hidden truth."

(Steve Anderson, Exec Producer: *"Faking It - Tears of a Crime"*)

"Best-in-class books on equity analysis invariably have a few pages dedicated to analysing human behaviour in an attempt to help the analysts decode the underlying meaning of corporate communications - more often than not perpetuating misconceptions about body language or other behavioural 'give-aways'. This book is a long needed methodical approach that facilitates and supports a structured and objective analysis of human behaviour, making it applicable in the field of equity analysis and investment management in general. Analysts and fund managers that start using the tools described in this book will quickly find themselves better equipped to understand the true meaning of corporate communications, and thereby empowered to make better investment decisions."

(Kristina Ganea, Fund Manager)

Cliff and his team have worked for three years with me and the Dutch Armed Forces. This book and SCAnR makes a significant contribution to those working in high-risk security contexts and will help Special Forces professionals with their judgments regarding the credibility of their interviewees. This is often in time critical and life threatening contexts.

(Major Tim Bosma, Head Education and Training Group Communication and Engagement. Dutch Armed Forces, NLD)

"Understanding the teaching contained in this book has helped me in two ways. Firstly, it taught me to look for the truth as opposed to flat out lies, thereby turning upside down what I have been doing for years making my investigative skills slicker. Secondly, being able to deconstruct what's in front of me to be able to put my finger on why I believe or disbelieve it, and then getting on to evidence it. This is so very important for front-line law enforcement officers as it could mean the difference between gaining the trust of a victim and successfully prosecuting the perpetrator."

(Luke Breakspear – Serving Police Inspector)

"While I would argue with Cliff about some of the specifics, I endorse not only the goal of this work but also the value of learning about it. There is much to gain here."

(Paul Ekman PhD)

Acknowledgements

Getting to the Truth is dedicated to the team at the *Emotional Intelligence Academy* (the EIA Group). They are a group of professionals[1] who came together in 2008 to widen and extend research, consultancy, and training in this field. They developed SCAnR© (Six Channel Analysis -Realtime) which is at the core of this scientific approach to behaviour analysis.

I thank the partners, consultants, and clients from business/banking/ insurance/investment sectors across the globe who have allowed us to develop, pilot and test this research in their high-stake environments. More recently I have enjoyed growing relationships with government and military clients where the ability to distinguish truth from lies could mean the difference between life and death for themselves, and the people they protect.

This was led by two of the research and development Directors at the EIA Group:

1. Aaron Garner MSc, who completed a huge part of the literary review and research behind SCAnR. He has also led or supported many of the SCAnR based piloting projects with me for our military, security and business sector clients around the globe.

2. Professor Dawn Archer, has worked tirelessly with her colleagues in the *University of Central Lancashire*(UCLan) and more recently with *Manchester Metropolitan University*(MMU) in helping the EIA Group to build a professional pathway for Behaviour Analysts through to PhD level via a Master of Science (MSc) Degree at MMU – the *MSc in Communications, Behaviour and Credibility Analysis*. This has enabled a multi-discipline approach which extends opportunities for our behaviour analyst related clients and students into criminology, psychology, sociology, forensic linguistics, commercial and technology fields.

In 2010, we were honoured to receive the support of the pioneer in emotion and deception research, Dr Paul Ekman[2] - Professor Emeritus at the *University of California San Francisco*. Paul has dedicated his life to making the world a safer and more compassionate place – evidenced by the research he has published, the books he has written, the people he has inspired, the results he has achieved and the courses he has developed. He served as the scientific adviser to FOX Entertainment Group who produced a dramatisation of his work in the hit TV series '*Lie to Me*', in which he was characterised as Dr Cal Lightman -

11

played by Tim Roth. More recently he consulted with Disney/Pixar on 'Inside Out'[3] their animated film about emotions. He has also created powerful online training to help convert his research into practical tools that develop skills to read micro-facial expressions, and knowledge of how to respond effectively to others in the home, at work and in law enforcement.

Paul, through his company *Paul Ekman Group LLC*, agreed to partner with us at the EIA Group in 2010 under a company we named *Paul Ekman International plc* (PEI).[4] This was central to furthering the shared goals of contributing more widely towards global compassion and to world safety and security.

The reason for detailing this association is to credit Dr Paul Ekman unreservedly for his openness and support over the last seven years. Our association has been, and is, a great platform for the research, training, development and consultancy work we are doing across and beyond PEI and the EIA Group. I also want to say a special thank you to his Vice President, John Pearse PhD, for sharing his experience, mentorship and friendship over the same period. He has been generous in sharing his time and knowledge with me from his experience as a psychologist, author[5] and experienced counter-terrorism expert at Scotland Yard.

I would also like to thank Dr Leanne ten Brinke[6], Professor Stephen Porter[7], Dr Mary Schollum[8] and Dr Clea Wright Whelan[9] for their contributions in their own right and their support of our research.

I must stress, though, that the views and opinions expressed in this book are mine, and may not necessarily represent those of any of these individuals, or the organisations they represent.

I owe much of my development in emotional intelligence to my three children, Jordan, Harry and Keaton who have tested, challenged, developed and warmed me with their personalities, escapades, love and 'feedback'.

And finally to my friend, my love, my mentor, and my wife for 33 years. Ellen keeps my conscience and my heart in the right place whenever they start to wobble in my interactions with others.

Introduction

"Throughout any of this... Ian... was there any occasion where you actually came into contact... physical contact... with the girls?"

A police officer posed this question to Ian Huntley during a video recorded interview. Huntley was a school caretaker suspected of being involved with the disappearance of two ten-year-old friends, Holly Wells and Jessica Chapman on 4 August 2002 in Cambridgeshire, UK.

Huntley replied, *"Physical contact? No."*

On the face of it, this may seem like a reasonable answer and may not appear to be helpful in ascertaining the truth in such an investigation. But when you explore this short twelve-second interaction using the **SCAnR** approach (**S**ix **C**hannel **An**alysis - **R**ealtime) you find 12 clues in and around Huntley's three words that suggest we may not be dealing with the truth here.

We'll look in detail at the SCAnR approach shortly and explore how it relates to this and other episodes. You will see how it has been applied by us, and other behaviour analysts we have trained, in high-stake crime, security, intelligence, investment and negotiation scenarios to help differentiate lies from truth.[10]

I have provided links to audio and video examples of the points being made. These can all be found in the online resource library at: www.gettingtothetruth.com. These will help you to review and practice your skills as you move through the book.

For the moment, though, pause and consider the following simple statement. What does it mean... exactly?

"It's cold in here".

Cameron, my business partner, and friend, would say bluntly that it means s/he feels cold, and imply I was silly for even asking.

On the other hand, my wife Ellen would say that _"it depends"_, and she would add that if I want to know the true meaning then I need to consider the context, the tone of voice, the emphasis within the phrase, the accompanying body language and gestures, and the genuine or posed emotions transmitted through the speaker's facial expressions.

I point out the distinctions in their approaches to highlight that we all have choices in our communication exchanges. We can take the written or spoken words from others at face value, or we can be curious and look more deeply behind the words, if we are interested in what they are really thinking and feeling, whatever their utterances.

The true meaning of the statement could be that it's a simple statement of fact, or a criticism about the ambient temperature or the social atmosphere. It may be a hint from a house guest to get you to turn up the heating. Or it might be a positive statement from someone who needs a chilled environment to carry out an experiment or store food. The point is that the words themselves are only the tip of the iceberg.

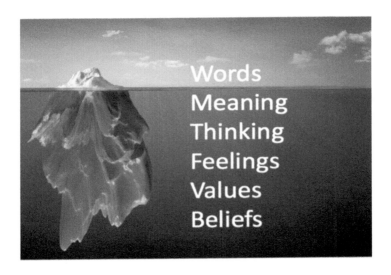

Figure 1: Iceberg of Meaning

Let's take a few more examples where the words and the meaning may differ. Think for a moment of a few interpretations of each of these following phrases. Assume that they are said to you by a close friend, or from your spouse or domestic partner:

1. "Are you hungry?"

2. "I hate you"

3. "Go ahead".

The first statement could be a genuine interest in your need for food, or it could be a hint that he/she would like to eat something. It may be a hint for you to prepare it for them. Or to take her/him out for a meal. It could be a sarcastic remark towards you as you overindulge in too much food. The second statement could be an angry attack or it could be an affectionate phrase whilst inside she/he is thinking, "I really love this man/woman". And the third may not be permission!

If you have suggested something that may be a little selfish then this could be a dare. Don't do it!

Tone of voice, the face and body, and other factors usually guide you towards meaning ... if you are being attentive.

Understanding what is going on below the waterline of the iceberg can be so valuable in forming and maintaining constructive relationships. We often depend on each other for safety, security, work projects, services and friendship, and so the ability to read and understand others can help you to enrich and enhance such relationships.

The good news is that many of the skills involved in reading others are innate – you were born with them. The even better news is that you can learn the ones that aren't built-in, and develop the ones that are natural. This book is designed to help you on that journey.

In **Getting to the Truth** the core skill is about noticing what you see and hear, including, but not restricted to, the words that are offered to you.

Some of the guidance I will offer here may be at odds with myths and theories you may have read in other books to do with reading people, body language, facial expressions, and interviewing techniques. This may be due to some approaches being written for entertainment. Others may be poorly researched, or simply result from the interests, passion and experience of those who are representative of specific sectors, or who promote specific applications.

In this book I will cover the skills needed to spot the clues by using reliable approaches based on good research. I will:

- steer you away from the myths and towards the science and hard evidence in recognising the truth, reading emotions and in detecting deception.

- avoid the 'snake-oil' claims and approaches that only use one or two elements – like *cognitive load*[11], just facial expressions and body language, or only language, or solely the voice, or total reliance on biometrics(e.g. polygraphs). Each of these approaches, used alone, are risky and unreliable[12].

- employ a multi-channel, corroborative approach[13] to help you towards reliable decision making.

Many books and articles often claim that *'research suggests'* without supporting that claim with a reference we can follow to validate it.

So I will also validate the approaches I offer by adding **endnotes** at the back of the book, to provide links for you to follow if and when you become interested in answering the question, "*Who says?*".

These endnotes will allow you – whether you are a fellow geek, a security/business professional, a student or just a curious reader – to dig more deeply into areas that may be relevant to your own interests, work or research. My aim is to help bridge the gap between practical and effective real-world applications, and the underpinning academic research.

If you are not interested in people, or curious about what others may be thinking or feeling, or you are disillusioned by the many contradictions in this field of work then please stick with it for a while. I believe I can stimulate that interest a little and dispel the myths for you.

Step by step

There are three parts to this book, each with short sections you can dip into and come back to as needed.

Part One sets the scene around how to get to the truth and digs into the secrets and fallacies around truth and lie detection.

Part Two is the behavioural analysis section that outlines the SCAnR system and details the important elements of the six communication channels shown here in Figure 2:

Figure 2: Six channels of communication

The audio and video examples are there for you to test your skills if you choose to. I would encourage you to do this.

The other key skill in getting to the truth is about the questions and probes you use. These are very difficult skills to develop using the printed word as they rely on face-to-face interaction and practice. However, I will start to open up this aspect in <u>Part Three</u>, where I will introduce some key principles and tips on how to manage your interactions with others.

A Glossary of Terms, used within the behavioural analysis field, is included for you as Appendix 3. You may find it useful as you come across terms you're unsure of during your wider reading, or where I haven't explained things very well in this book.

Lies come in various forms and can be totally fabricated stories similar in theme to the ones below:

- "We must do coffee sometime!"

- "Of course I love you!"

- "No, your bottom doesn't look big in that dress".

- "Sorry I am late. The traffic was so busy this morning!"

- "I did not have sexual relations with that woman!"

- "It wasn't me, honestly!"

- "I left my last job because I wanted more of a challenge!"

They can also be exaggerations (e.g. "The fish that got away was one metre long!"). Or they can be concealments or omissions. For example, a person might describe her journey home from work to her partner and completely miss out the short visit to her lover on the way. This is lying too. A *lie* is defined by Dr Paul Ekman as 'a deliberate attempt to mislead, without prior notification'. This is set against *truth* which he suggests is a 'sincere attempt to provide accurate information.'[14]

The last three words in the *lie* definition help us to eliminate magicians, negotiators, poker players, undercover agents and actors from the label as in these cases it is mostly accepted that:

- the magic is a trick to entertain,

- your sad reaction to a dealt card that you need is a bluff,

- your 'best price' isn't your best price,

- deception is authorised for national security reasons, and

- you aren't really 'Batman' as you are Ben Affleck playing a part in a movie.

What we do know, that is very useful when we need to get to the truth, is that lies will most likely:

1. be linked with emotions;

2. require greater cognitive effort than truthful messages;

3. be associated with arousal; and

4. prompt liars to over-control their behaviours.[15]

I recommend that you pause here for a moment and re-read these four factors as they represent themes that underpin most of the better research.

So let's start with a brief look into emotion and thought.

In truth and lie detection it is important to try to work out what others are feeling and thinking

Paul Ekman PhD, the pioneer of emotion research, suggests that emotions help us to deal with matters of importance to our welfare, without thinking.[16]

The Power of Emotions

Core emotions such as fear, anger, sadness, happiness, disgust, contempt and surprise can happen to us within half a second of something triggering them. The resulting impulse linked to each of these emotions sets off its own orchestrated, synchronised array of physiological changes across our body to help us to deal with the universal triggers of each emotion. Simultaneous changes in, for example:

- heart rate

- blood pressure

- breath rate

- voice (e.g. volume, pitch and speed of speech)

- local blood circulation and temperature

- muscular/body tension, freezing and movements

- digestion system (de)activation

- facial expressions

- eye movement, closure, blinking and pupil size

- perspiration.

The fact that this impulse happens within around 400 milliseconds (two fifths of a second) of the trigger, even before the conscious mind is aware that we are in the grip of an emotion[17], is a gift to the behaviour analyst. This includes poker players, lovers, negotiators, salespeople and interviewers who may need to determine what someone is really feeling. It can also be a major problem for the undercover agents, police, and air marshals that we work with whose lives may depend on them getting away with a false cover story to keep their nations safe.

Such *emotional leakage* from humans can often be seen and heard, without technological aids, even if someone wants to mask or hide the emotion they are feeling.

Here lies the beauty of *homo sapiens*, in that we have evolved to automatically show and recognise these indicators of emotion to help us, and our compatriots, to thrive and build constructive relationships, and also to survive against predators and threats.[18]

Felt emotions are innate, unbidden, brief and they are shared by our predecessors, primates, and many animals. We can see them as a gift – guardians – that steer us through life and protect us from harm.

The good news is that good information and training, starting with books like this, can help us to identify what it is we see and hear, so we can make informed, reliable judgments about our thinking, actions, and decision

Emotional Intelligence

This is central to the wider concept of **emotional intelligence** that is about **awareness, understanding and influencing self and others** and is probably best illustrated with the three-by-three grid in Figure 3.

I believe this captures the key elements of the various emotional intelligence frameworks[19] used in this field:

	Awareness	Understanding	Influence
Self	Physiological sensations and thoughts	Trigger, impulse, evolved reaction, potential impact	Self-management
Context	Macro and micro factors	Impact on behaviour	Context management
Other	Account, baseline and cross-channel data consistencies	Intended message, semantics, thinking, feeling and values	Interaction/ relationship management

Figure 3: Emotional Intelligence Matrix
(© Emotional Intelligence Academy Ltd [2013])

Awareness of our emotions, the context of the interaction and others' emotions is step one (the 'Awareness' column).

Understanding what is going on is outlined in the middle column, and **Influencing** or acting on this insight is covered in the right-hand column.

Remember, though, that these signals work both ways in that we display these physiological changes too, and others can pick up on that.

Imagine you have applied for a job you are not quite qualified to do, and you decide to embellish your résumé to help you secure the job. Even an inexperienced interviewer may pick up that 'there is something not quite right' from your behaviour, but they just can't put their finger on it. Emotional load such as fear, i.e. the fear of being caught in a lie, often leaks, without our awareness. As can the fear of being disbelieved, or the stress of an interview - and these are often confused with each other.

Paul Ekman coined the phrase *Othello Error* in his book Telling Lies, linked to Shakespeare's play (Othello). It refers to the look on Desdemona's face following an accusation from Othello that she was having an affair with Cassio and that Othello had claimed he had killed him.[20] She was actually experiencing the despair of being disbelieved, with no means to prove otherwise, not weeping for the loss of a lover.

Liars can also feel guilty or shameful when lying to loved ones. They can get also pleasure from getting away with a lie (e.g. in poker).

Such emotional leakage, therefore, does not necessarily mean deception, as we will explore again later. So I will call these signals *Points of Interest* or **'PIns'**.

One **PIn** alone does not mean we have found a lie. What is interesting is the moment when we discover...

...three or more PIns across two or more communication channels within seven seconds of a stimulus or question.[21]

Clusters of PIns give you a strong indication of deception if you have eliminated the many other causes of leakage such as anxiety, habits, and discomfort. I will guide you on how to do that later.

Psychological Model of Lies

As well as emotional load, we can also experience cognitive load when we lie. The relationship between cognition and emotion is a key feature of the 'psychological model for lies' in Figure 4 below.

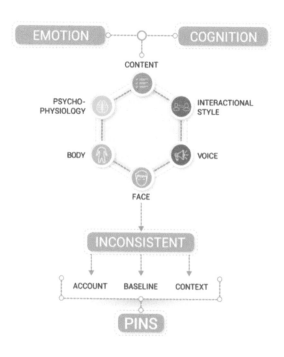

Figure 4: Psychological Model for Lies
(adapted from Pearse, J. and Lansley, C.A. (2010)[22])

When we are truthful there is spontaneity, consistency, flow and harmony between what we are thinking and feeling. When we lie, our emotion and cognition domains are more likely to collide – to clash – thereby creating a competition for resources.

This often results in leakage from one or more of the six communication channels:

- Interactional Style (the way we say or write our words and phrases)

- Voice (the 'music' of the voice including pitch, volume and tone)

- Verbal Content (what we say or write)

- Face (expressions seen in bulges, creases and furrows resulting from movements of one or more of the 43 muscles of the face)

- Body (movements of everything else except what is covered by face)

- Psychophysiology (changes within the body that can sometimes show externally – even without biometric apparatus – such as perspiration and breath rate).

This leakage is very interesting when it is inconsistent with the **ABC**'s. This refers to the other person's:

- **Account** (i.e., the story s/he is trying to convey)

- their apparent/emerging **Baseline** behaviour, and

- **Context** (the influence of the immediate *micro* setting (e.g. the interview) and the wider *macro* context of culture, politics, events, etc.).

Such inconsistencies are PIns.

Truth Leakage

We usually have to work harder when we are lying – we have to remember more - and the more important the occasion, the higher the stakes or the more serious the consequences, the more likely that the truth will leak out when we are lying.[23]

Figure 5: When people lie - they leak the truth.

For those reading this book with the intention of becoming better liars, here is the problem. Yes, this book will probably make you a better liar, but you won't be able to fool those who are trained, or other readers of this book. The reason will be revealed if you can bear with me for a moment.

Let's first explore the timeline of an emotional episode so that you can see how most of this leakage can happen before we are conscious of it.

If we use an example of a threat of harm, such as the sight or sound of something resembling a snake, then this will trigger the emotion of fear in many of us including the following effects:

- we will freeze,

- our heart rate will increase,

- our eyes will widen,

- our brows will rise and squeeze together,

- our mouth will stretch sideways,

- blood will flow away from the surface of the skin and towards the essential organs and large muscles in the legs preparing us to run – though once aware of the situation, we may not choose to do so.

This is the amazing autonomic (sympathetic) nervous system at work.

Stimuli such as loss of gravity and large objects moving toward us are usually picked up automatically and take what neuroscientist, Joseph LeDoux, calls the 'quick and dirty low road' in the brain from the hypothalamus to the amygdala.[24] This results in physiological changes or impulses within our body in less than half a second.

This is illustrated by the 'React/Respond Model' in Figure 6.

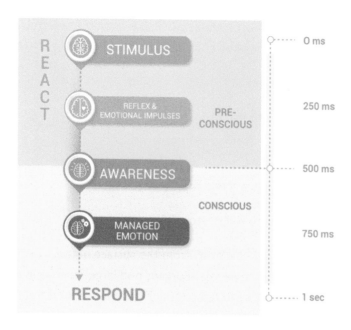

Figure 6: React/Respond Model

The precise timing is still being debated by neuroscientists, though for our purposes all we need to know is that these impulses fall within the pre-conscious zone and seem to be far too quick for us to interfere with. Awareness within an emotional episode will take around half a second or more, often a second or two, after the stimulus or trigger.

Sometimes we only become aware of being emotional when someone tells us we are being so, several seconds or minutes later! Emotions are powerful.

'Emotional systems tend to monopolize brain resources,' said LeDoux[25]. 'It's much easier for an emotion to control a thought than for a thought to control an emotion.'

Logic and rational thinking can get pushed aside. This means that reactions from an emotional impulse can result in emotional behaviour that we later regret; though often these reactions are there to serve us, save our life, build relationships and motivate behaviour.[26] Once we become aware of the impulse and its associated trigger it can help us to reflect quickly on whether the *reaction* is appropriate or whether it may be wiser to choose a different *response*.

I was working with a group a few years ago when a member of the group shared that she had a great tip that she had learned from a coach who was helping her with the anger control element of her Asperger's condition[27]. The tip was to 'count to one' at the point she realised she was becoming angry. I had heard of the ten-second version of this, though this highlighted how short a time she felt she needed to reflect, and then choose a response to help her with her social interactions.

Remember though that 'managing emotions' does not always mean suppressing them or becoming 'unemotional'. Emotions are designed to serve our wellbeing and our social interactions, and in many situations the outward expression of emotions that you are feeling is good for you, and for those you care about.

There are times though when our evolved reactions from emotion can be counter-productive.

For example:

1. Fear can make us freeze. This served our primates well if they were being hunted by an animal or an enemy in the wilderness. It didn't work too well for one of my sons who recently came off his motorcycle on a main highway. He recalled freezing for 'what felt like a full minute' whilst he lay on the ground, a little shaken, in the middle lane. It took him a while to interrupt this automatic reaction as he became aware of the oncoming traffic and he scrambled to the safety of the edge of the road.

2. Anger can overpower rational thought and cause us to overreact with those we care about.

3. Anger and fear can also impede the performance of those involved in competitive and combat sports as they 'lose control'.

It can also impede our ability to stay in the moment and be ultra-attentive when we need to focus on the behavioural impulses and sensations from within and the emotional signals from others.

Being attentive

This brings us to the crucial skill for getting to the truth and effective social interaction. The ability to be attentive to relevant data or signals coming from across the six communication channels, simultaneously.

I have three tips for you here:

1. **Assume truth**: be alerted only by the signals from others that are reliable indicators that they may not be being truthful.

2. **Be curious:** stay non-judgemental and seek to fully understand what the other person is thinking and feeling.

3. **Be mindful**: Stay focused in the present moment.

Let's look at each of these in a little more depth.

1. Assume truth

It is good practice to collect all data coming from humans, without filtering, and consider those signals in depth, using slow motion video replays and other technology where we can. Unfortunately, in most real-world situations, this is not feasible, and so this is where we take a major leap with our approach and we **assume truth**.

I know... I know. The psychologists and researchers amongst you might be screaming right now that "This is a bias!". You are right. In our research labs and in consultancy contexts where this is possible, we do gather data, consider hypotheses and evaluate it clinically using detailed codes to scrutinise which muscle groups are moving in the face and measuring the decibels of the voice to pick up volume changes, and so on.

Many professionals, behaviour analysts and others reading this book are probably working out in the field, on their own, real-time. In relationships and friendships this is the context too. Unfortunately, we cannot bring our portable laboratory into most of our social settings – even those that are high-stake. And I would not choose to as I prefer not to contaminate the interactions I do with overt equipment such as thermal cameras, biometric equipment and audio/video recorders if I can avoid it. I realise that there is a place for covert monitoring of humans from a distance, and technology is helping that a great deal, though that then brings the issue of ethics, protocol and legislation into play.

You do not need permission to bring eyes, ears and behaviour analysis skills into any interview room or social setting (yet!). In time, in certain contexts, I guess there may be a need for disclosure of such capabilities to be pure on the ethics front.

What we are learning from our experience and research[28] is that it can help an individual to perform real-time if they assume individuals are honest, and we ignore truthful signals. The bulk of our clients have to work in this real-world 'street-fighter' environment – working alone and in real-time with no replays. So this can help in several ways:

1. It allows us to be attentive to the research-corroborated deception indicators (PIns) that could be worthy of revisiting with questions later, especially where they leak out in clusters.

2. Liars often embed their lies within the truth as part of their attempts to convince you that they are truthful. Paying too much attention to the truth will drain your resources and may bias your judgment, causing you to

miss the reliable signs of deception if and when they occur. If they don't appear, then you are probably looking at the truth[29].

3. It prevents us being overwhelmed by data that the short-term and working memory will struggle to capture, hold and process on-the-fly, especially if the context doesn't allow us to take notes or make recordings.

Let me give you a practical example, focused just on the visual channel.

Exercise: Please pause from reading this book for a moment and consider your surroundings for around 15 seconds and notice the detail of everything you can see. Then list down what you noticed. Go on... please try it.

The chances are that you will be able to recall many items, though the detail may be fairly general, especially if the surroundings are unfamiliar to you.

Now, scan the environment again for 15 seconds but pay attention to the details of only the things that are red (or shades of red) in colour.

Again note down afterward what you can recall from the 15-second scanning. Off you go.

It is likely that you were drawn quickly to target red items (assuming there are some!) and you will have paid more attention to the detail – the sizes, textures, colour tones, material, etc. You may have less detail about anything that isn't red which you didn't need your attention.

In a similar way many people report that they suddenly notice dozens of cars like their own when they newly acquire a certain model or make of car.

This selective attentiveness can ease the strain and your cognitive load[30] by allowing you to filter in useful information for truth/lie detection and filter out the less useful data (known as 'distractors').

Trying to take in all multichannel data can be like drinking water from a fire hose, and this can create data-overload, as illustrated by Figure 7.

Figure 7: Data-overload

Working with others, real-time, needs a strategy that helps you to remove the 'noise' of the thousands of pieces of data that are reaching your senses. Otherwise you risk overload and ineffectiveness when you are trying to understand others.

2. Be curious

Suspending judgment about a person helps in two ways. It can help you to stay in an investigative mode so that you can stay open to multi-channel signals. Secondly, it prevents you from leaking emotions such as disgust, anger and contempt that may be picked up on by the other person.

This can be a problem during investigative interviews where a guilty suspect may react to such judgments about them with shame, and this may cause them to close up as they consider how they will be viewed by friends, family and the public.

When a guilty individual is being interviewed, a skilled behavior analyst will focus in a non-oppressive manner on the *act,* as a mistake or a wrong deed, without minimalising a crime, and steer the conversation to allow the guilty suspect to release the pressure of guilt through a confession so they can move forward together.

3. Be mindful

The greatest compliment that I believe you can show someone is to give them your 100%, undivided attention. This is also a powerful approach if you wish to optimise your performance in really understanding others or spotting if they are lying to you.

I applaud those who believe that they can multi-task, though I would advise against this practice for real-time people-reading. Specifically, I am referring to the process of observing and, at the same time, preparing or asking your next question.

It is very difficult, especially when working alone, to pay attention to all six channels and think about your next question at the same time. One interferes with the other.

To prove this to yourself, try this next exercise for a few seconds.

Exercise: Before you turn the page, think about the design of the Eiffel Tower whilst simultaneously thinking about your detailed schedule for tomorrow - step by step.

Almost impossible...

It seems that we are only able to process one piece of information at one time so what I often find when I challenge people with this exercise is that most people report that they flick back and forth, very quickly, between the two processes. This dilutes or splits our focus and will interfere with our performance as behaviour analysts.

So, if you have to perform both roles alone, I recommend that when you are observing others you avoid any other physical or mental processes. Simply focus on the 'now' and watch and listen. This is called mindfulness. For those interested in a cost-effective, secular introduction to this discipline you may wish to look up the mindfulness guru, Jon Kabat Zinn. There are many other approaches available via the internet and there is a module focused on attentiveness on the EIA Group website[31] too.

In brief, Jon Kabat Zinn suggests that mindfulness is about paying attention, on purpose, in the present moment, without judgment, as if our life depends on it.[32]

So this means focusing on the now, second by second when others are interacting with you, and managing the temptations to re-process what you have just heard in the past or think about where you are going in the future. Athletes and sporting competitors report that when they are focused on the now, in the zone, they perceive time to slow down and this allows them to perform at an optimal level.

Wayne Gretsky, the famous ice hockey player says that he doesn't skate to where the puck is – he skates to where it's going to be. Commentators would often say that Gretzky seemed to be two seconds ahead of everyone else. Many put this down to his experience that enabled him to predict the play and some described it a luck.

He describes that his moment by moment awareness was key, and this came from what he saw combined with the sound of skates on the ice around him that told him the proximity and speed of his team mates and competitors.[33]

Some more good news here. Mindfulness can be learned. By focusing on an automatic process, such as our own breath going in and out of our body, we can discipline the mind to pay attention to our automatic emotions and impulses, as well as those signals from others. And don't worry. This is not about religion, lotus positions on the floor, or eight weeks in a cave; mindfulness is something that can be achieved within a few minutes with a little practice.

I use a visual metaphor of 'settling the sand'. On my desk I have a plastic container full of water with a small amount of sand in it. I experimented to find the right sand that settles within two minutes and here are the images of my container (left to right)... after shaking... one minute later... then after two minutes. I imagine the sand particles as representing past and future thoughts that I need to quieten to get myself in the moment.

I don't need to carry this around with me now, as I can visualize the stages over the two minutes, without the prop, and can get into a mindful state very quickly.

For those who haven't enjoyed the benefits of meditation and mindfulness I can highly recommend the books and approaches by Jon Kabat-Zinn.[34]

You may even be inspired to explore the wider benefits of mindfulness, in addition to maximizing your potential as a behavior analyst, by considering the evidence signposted by the American Psychological Association.[35]

Clusters of PIns

Most researchers working in the area of truth and lie detection agree that there is no *Pinocchio's Nose*, no single indicator of deception. Be careful, therefore, not to jump to conclusions when you notice just one signal. This is so tempting.

If you do feel yourself pre-judging from single signals, stereotypes, prejudice, or what we call 'Me Theory' (judging others' actions from your perspective, e.g. 'If I were him I would be sad right now'), and other biases, then go and find yourself a newspaper, roll it up and tap yourself on the shoulders twice whilst simultaneously saying 'bad dog...bad dog'! Keep the newspaper handy – bias happens to the best of us. We are cognitive misers (lazy thinkers who can take short cuts) and so the newspaper may serve as a reminder for you in those moments of low self-discipline. You will then be on your way to join good researchers and experienced practitioners in this field who support the idea of **clusters** of behavioural indicators[36].

Clusters help us to cross-check or corroborate evidence across communication channels towards more reliable judgements. I will go a little further and offer a working definition of a *cluster* as a guide to prevent you from over-reacting to a single indicator, or a couple of indicators from the same communication channel.

So I define a cluster using the **'3-2-7 Rule'** which is:

3 PIns across 2 or more channels within 7 seconds
of the meaning point of a stimulus/question.

I have seen great results[37] from those who can be totally attentive to others for around seven seconds after a stimulus is presented to a person.

In most cases, by 'stimulus', I am referring to an unexpected question or probe from an interviewer. However, the stimuli in security and law enforcement contexts could also include:

- tactical use of evidence or images of evidence,

- the strategic positioning of yellow-jacketed, uniformed officials at major sports events, or

- the engagement of a 'sniffer dog' in an airport.

By 'meaning point' of a question, by the way, I mean the point at which a person can predict the purpose of the question being asked. Let's take the question asked of Huntley again.

"Throughout any of this... Ian... was there any occasion where you actually came into contact... physical contact... with the girls?"

You can see later that at this point Huntley was squirming in his seat. He seemed to have gathered this was going to be a challenging probe when the detective mentioned his name, mid-sentence, and he probably would have grasped where she was going with this question the moment she uttered the words 'contact... physical contact' even though she hadn't completed her question.

This is the point where the attentiveness clock of the interviewer needs to start ticking, usually for a couple of seconds as the question tails off and for a further five seconds after the question finishes. During these seven seconds all radars need to be on, and past and future thinking needs to be quietened to allow this present-time, in the moment, attentiveness.

The second reason for this seven-second concentration is that it is highly likely that the responses and behaviours from the other person will be associated with the stimulus during this period. After that time the skilled liars are likely to take you to areas where they are more comfortable and away from what you are interested in.[38]

If you are working as a pair or a team, then the roles can be divided though the bulk of situations faced by our clients involve them working alone. This is often the case in the non-security settings too such as selling, performance reviews, negotiations and personal relationships. If you suspect your partner is cheating on you, it might be a little intrusive to suggest to her/him that you would like your colleague to join you while you have a little chat.

Like any skill, this kind of attentiveness needs practice and it is useful to practice channel-by-channel. You can do this once you have completed Part Two of this book where I will go through all the *Pins* with you.

Before I move into the six channels and the PIns, I have an ethical message for you. What you learn here will help you to read what others are thinking and feeling; often those 'others' may not want you to have that insight, for many good as well as bad reasons. Once you have developed this capability I am afraid that you may find that you can't turn it off.

If the stakes are high and you have a duty or responsibility to access and act on this information, then this will greatly enhance your effectiveness. Most of the time though, you may have to resist the excitement of acting on the deep truths that you see and hear. Especially with friends and family. Otherwise you will create distance between them and you. More times than not, therefore, I would suggest that it is better to believe a lie and trust people - and occasionally be let down or hurt – and simply arm yourself with the approaches in this book, and save them for when the stakes are high so you pick up the serious stuff. Much healthier, I believe, than disbelieving truths and living your life as a defensive cynic. It's bad Karma.

It can be healthy to take the view that 98% of the world are good people who tell the truth most of the time. Some of us may be guilty of occasionally performing bad deeds, but most people, most of the time, are caring, compassionate and honest.

OK, OK... no endnotes here as I have no scientific proof for this statistic. And I confess that I am no angel. I am not able to maintain this perspective all the time. This is simply a mantra that helps me to:

Become curious about why people do cruel or bad things, rather than respond with natural, primal emotion and judge them or act with contempt, disgust, anger or hatred.

I may be kidding myself, but I find this gives me a better, attentive, non-judgemental mindset that helps me when I engage with others. This is especially important when involved in investigative interviews. If the suspect or perpetrator senses that they are being judged, rather than understood, they may close-up and make my job of getting to the truth so much harder.

Video Exercise

I would now like to go back to the example phrases that I used at the start of the book:

"Physical contact? No."

On paper these are merely words. It is difficult to establish meaning from this single dimension, especially without any context. Real meaning becomes clearer when we can hear the speaker's tone, volume, pitch and phrasing. It's even better when we can also see the person speaking alongside his/her body language and facial expressions.

If you can access the internet, let's add a few dimensions to the second phrase and see/hear what stands out for you using the following link to the short Police interview that was broadcasted on UK television as part of a programme where I served as a behaviour analysis consultant.[39]

The video (VIDEO 1 at www.gettingtothetruth.com) features Ian Huntley, a school caretaker suspected of being involved with the disappearance of two ten-year-old friends, Holly and Jessica, in the UK (2002). He is being interviewed here by a female police officer.

Play the video once and record what you notice.

Figure 8 outlines a summary of the key data over the 12-second long video with 'PIn Codes' that will be explained following this exercise.

You may have noticed:

Secs	Script	Huntley 'Points of Interest'(PIns)	PIn Codes
0 to 7 secs	Detective: "Throughout any of this... Ian... was there any occasion where you actually came into contact... physical contact... with the girls?"	Liplick – dry mouth. Mouth muscle tension (and swallow?). Eye closure. (Body repositioning is ignored) Lean back.	P6 B4 (P6?) B5 B1
8 to 11 secs	Huntley: "Physical contact?..No."	Grab arm(tension/control). Manipulators increase(hand rub). Evasion? (repeats question back). Misunderstand simple question? (answers before she repeats it back). Volume down on 'no'. Single sided shoulder shrug. Eye closure. Head shake not in sync with word 'no'.	B4 B3 S2 S2 V2 B1 B5 B1
12 secs	Detective: "OK".		

Figure 8: Huntley Points of Interest

52

From a 3-word response we have 12 Points of Interest, or PIns, from Huntley's Body, Voice, Interactional Style and Psychophysiology. 8 of these Pins were from across 3 channels within 7 seconds of the stimulus; in this case the meaning point ('physical contact') of the question. You may have noticed some of these, though don't worry if you didn't get them all, as the tips on spotting these comes later. It is highly unusual by the way, when people are being **truthful**, to have such a large cluster of potential deception indicators, across communication channels, within such a short period of time. But this isn't unusual when they are **lying**[40].

Once you become familiar with the 27 criteria across the six channels you will be surprised at how often you notice them when people lie – especially in high-stake situations.

So let's move on to the 27 criteria organised under each of these six channels.

First, here's an overview of the 27 criteria for you.

(N.B. I have also included references [e.g. S1/V2/P3] in parenthesis below. We use these for shorthand in our research and coding work).

Interactional Style:

- Flow (S1)

- Evasiveness (S2)

- Impression management (S3)

Voice:

- Volume (V1)

- Pitch (V2)

- Tone (V3)

Verbal Content:

- Tense (C1)

- Distancing (C2)

- Statement analysis (C3)

- Verbal slip (C4)

Facial Expression:

- FACS[41] Anomaly (F1)

- Duration of the expression (F2)

- Symmetry across the face (F3)

- Synchrony between muscles (F4)

- Profile of the expression (F5)

Body Language:

- Gestural slip (B1)

- Illustrators (B2)

- Manipulators (B3)

- Tension (B4)

- Eyes (B5)

Psychophysiology:

- Heart rate (P1)

- Perspiration (P2)

- Temperature (P3)

- Blood pressure (P4)

- Breathing (P5)

- Digestion (P6)

- Pupils (P7).

The main research papers supporting these 27 criteria are listed for you in Appendix 2.

We will move on now to explore the criteria from the first channel - Interactional Style.

1. Interactional Style

This is about how we interact with others through words (in sentences or utterances). At the beginning of the book I highlighted that lies will most likely:

1.   be linked with emotions;

2.   require greater cognitive effort than truthful messages;

3.   be associated with arousal; and

4.   prompt liars to over-control their behaviours.[42]

When we tell a lie it can be hard work and result in changes to our normal style of communicating (our baseline for a given context). We have to (i) hide the truth we are trying to conceal, (ii) construct and fabricate a false story and (iii) remember what we have said already to make sure it is consistent with those previous accounts.

This creates what psychologists term, 'cognitive load'. We can also suffer 'emotional load' due to, for example, the fear of being caught in a lie or the guilt of lying to a loved one.

This strain can create leakage in the way we communicate in terms of:

- Flow (S1)

- Evasiveness (S2)

- Impression management (S3)

Flow

Cognitive load can result in disturbances in communication flow such as:

- Pauses – the silences and gaps during speech

- Filled pauses – utterances and phrases that are sometimes used to fill pauses (e.g. erm, urm, er, you know, at the end of the day, etc.)

- Stutters, disfluencies, hesitations and false starts ("Li...Like this")

- Avoidance of contractions – "I did not have sex with that woman..." rather than "I didn't..."

- Speed and rhythm changes.

The key here is that we are looking for behaviour **changes from baseline**. Remember that I define a PIn as a behavioural indicator from one of the six communication channels that is inconsistent with the Account, Baseline and/or Context.

Evasiveness

Evasiveness is often employed by politicians as well as by liars – especially when they want to avoid giving information (or committing themselves to that information). Liars will often conceal lies or avoid telling them by using similar avoidance strategies and tactics. This is especially the case when responding to a question that may reveal their lies. Potential strategies include the following:

- Claiming not to understand a simple question that was heard

- Using qualifiers as, for example, an exclusion tactic [*what I can say is..*], or to show a (limited) level of speaker commitment [*could/might*], etc.

- Avoiding an immediate direct denial when accused (e.g. avoiding saying "I didn't do it!")

- Defensiveness (e.g., attacking the questioner or the questioning process)

- Inappropriate impoliteness (e.g., 'You are an idiot to question me on this')

- Referral (to previous comment by self/other)

- Omission (ignoring or skipping over key point).

If you want to listen to a politician applying a little evasiveness, then you may wish to review one of the clips of Senator Weiner being questioned by journalists about his alleged tweeting of a lewd photograph to a young female follower. This is VIDEO 2 from the resource site: www.gettingtothetruth.com.

Impression management

When we tell the truth, and we feel others are believing us, all we need to do is tell the story. When we lie, we need to work harder at getting the target of our lie to believe us. Phil Houston and his colleagues put this succinctly in their book, *'Spy the Lie'*. They use the terms *Convey* and *Convince*. When we tell the truth the facts are our friend and we simply need to convey those facts. A liar, however, will often channel their efforts to convince you that they are a truth teller. This can include the following:

- Religious reference ('Honest to God', 'I am a good Muslim/Catholic/Other')

- Belief/Values reference ('I disagree with lying', 'I don't agree with violence towards women')

- Character reference ('Ask my mother/colleagues, they will tell you I am a good person')

- Credibility qualifier ('Trust me', 'To be honest', 'I am not lying!')

- Representational frame ('We teenagers are being misjudged!')

- Inappropriate politeness ('But Sir/Madam, I am trying to explain', 'I am so grateful to the police')

- Proof or evidence seeking tack ('You can't prove it', 'Where is the evidence?').

It may also take the form of symbols or dress. Mick Philpott and his wife, Mairead, were imprisoned for their involvement in burning down their own home in Derby, UK, which killed six children. At an 'emotional' press appeal on 16 May 2012 prior to his arrest he chose to wear his 'dog tags' (an indicator of military service) outside of his clothing for the first time (after many TV appearances where he did not). In this clip you will see this, along with a range of other tactics designed to give the impression that he was a 'good guy' and seemingly uninvolved in the tragedy. Two weeks later, the Philpotts were charged with their children's murders. On 2 April 2013, they were found guilty of manslaughter (along with their friend and neighbour, Paul Mosley).

See VIDEO 3 at www.gettingtothetruth.com.

Mick Philpott's 'convincing' behaviour scored badly against our 'Impression management' factors (and others that I will come to later).

In summary, evasiveness tactics can prove to be valuable indicators (i.e. Pins) when they don't fit with the 'ABCs' - the Account or the story being communicated, the Baseline or normal style of the individual and where the leakage can't be explained by the Context of the interaction.

Also remember the 3-2-7 cluster rule. Whilst we might be able to locate a number of PIns that seem inconsistent with the A,B,Cs during a long presentation we should avoid getting too excited unless we notice:

3 PIns across 2 or more channels within 7 seconds

of the meaning point of a stimulus/question.

Interactional Style Summary:
- Flow (S1)
- Evasiveness (S2)
- Impression management (S3)

2. Voice

This is the musical element of our speech and you can hear it no matter which language is being spoken. The criteria are:

- Volume (V1)

- Pitch (V2)

- Tone (V3)

There are other elements, though our research and experience haven't turned up anything valuable from outside these three key aspects of voice that convinces us to include them as an additional potential indicator (at least, as yet). We will start first with volume.

Volume

This is relates to the intensity of a sound (i.e., how loud or soft it is). It can be measured in decibels, though I like to calibrate voice on a five-point scale, 5 being extremely loud and 1 being very quiet. 3 is the baseline for the person I am listening to, in that context. During the early phase of an interaction I will attempt to mark that baseline volume of the person so I can track changes from it. When a person lies, the volume often decreases from the person's baseline. This has been explained by the fact that most people are taught that lies are bad and so the volume drop indicates a distancing from the lies we tell. Be careful though, as it also drops when someone is unsure or sad. Volume can also vary with emotion and the phase of the story so remember the ABC. Is the volume inconsistent with the Account, Baseline and Context? If so, it's a PIn.

Listen to Huntley's three words again and notice what happens to the volume when he says "No". Compare that volume to when he repeated back the words "Physical contact?".

(VIDEO 1 at www.gettingtothetruth.com)

Did you notice the volume drop? On my scale it lowered from a three to a one. We do have ground (or to be precise, judicial) truth here by the way. Huntley was convicted of murder and is serving life imprisonment and, from the evidence found, it is highly likely these murders would have involved 'physical contact' between the murderer and the two victims of this terrible crime.

Here is another example of volume drop from Kato Kaolin[43], who testified at the trial of his then friend, OJ Simpson, in the widely publicized court case in the USA. The prosecutor was attempting to prove Kaolin had a book deal about the case so that she could dismiss him from the trial.

Listen to this video clip – VIDEO 4 at www.gettingtothetruth.com - especially when he claims "don't wanna do a book' near the end of the clip.

This is an illustration of how the waveform reduces (gets narrower towards the horizontal axis with lower volume) in Figure 9 using a piece of laboratory software[44].

However, most people can clearly hear the drop in volume without such equipment between the first 3 words and the last two that I have overlaid for you here.

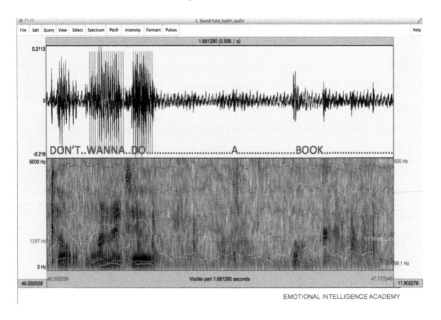

Figure 9: Kato Kaolin volume drop

N.B. the bottom half of this image is a spectrograph for the more detailed analysis often carried out in forensic work.

It was reported, later, that Kaolin had an informal arrangement with a writer named Marc Eliot[45] for a book.

Pitch is how high or low the 'note' of the speech is in the same way we have low notes and high notes on a piano. There is good research supporting the idea that pitch raises when people speak (or scream) as soon as they are first fearful or angry. Some people have questioned me on the latter, and suggest their own voice goes down when they want to project anger, e.g. to a child who is misbehaving.

The research holds good here though, as this example is likely to be a deliberate, conscious *performance*, rather than a pre-conscious *reaction* to a stimulus (i.e. it isn't a spontaneous, emotional reaction). The same applies to fear. Recall the screams on a roller-coaster – they are usually higher in pitch than a person's baseline. Again, I use a 5-point scale, with 3 being a person's baseline in that context, 5 being very high and 1 being very low pitch.

Knowing the voice profile of each of the emotions can help you to compare this indicator to the ABC in order to decide if you have a Pin here. Some research argues that the pitch goes up when we lie[46] though this is not strong enough to rely on in our view due to the other explanations for fear (e.g. being disbelieved, and anxiety from being interviewed).

Figure 10 outlines the current status of research[47] on voice in the form of a grid. You can see there is still some research work to do here.

Voice Research Summary

Factor	Pitch	Volume	Voice quality
Surprise	Increase*	No significant change*	?
Anger	Increase***	Increase***	'Edge'***
Fear	Increase**	Increase**/ Decrease*	?
Disgust	Decrease***	Decrease***	?
Contempt	Decrease***	Decrease***	?
Sad	Decrease***	Decrease***	'Soft'*
Happy	Increase***	Increase***	?
Deception	Increase*	Decrease***	?

Our subjective view on strength of research supporting each as universal indicator:
***Excellent/**Good/*Fair/?

Figure 10: Voice research summary

We should also keep in mind that pitch can be heavily determined by culture as well as gender and youth, so the key thing is that we are listening for changes from baseline.

Tone

And finally on this channel we have tone. This is the timbre or quality of the voice. It is everything except pitch and volume, that is, the characteristic that helps you identify a flute from a trumpet, for example, even though both are playing the same note at the same volume. As the grid in Figure 10 outlines in the third 'Voice quality' column, in sadness the voice is often *softer*. Also the slight rasp and *edge* in a voice can reveal the onset of anger in others.[48]

Voice Summary:
- Volume (V1)
- Pitch (V2)
- Tone (V3)

3. Verbal Content

The third channel is about the words we actually use. This is primarily focused on speech, though this also applies to letters, emails or even texts. The four criteria associated with Verbal Content are:

- Tense (C1)

- Distancing (C2)

- Statement analysis (C3)

- Verbal slip (C4)

Tense

This is about the inappropriate use of past, present, and future tense. A common example is when an individual uses the past tense when talking about someone they are arguing is alive.

An example is Mitchel Quy who confessed to, and was convicted of, murdering his wife, Lynsey. Before he was arrested he was interviewed on a TV programme where he slipped up by saying, "She WAS such a good mum' and then quickly corrected himself with, 'She IS such a good mum to the kids'. The clip is VIDEO 5 in the resource library - www.gettingtothetruth.com.

Quy had not questioned her mothering credentials (in the TV interview) prior to this, and so the first part of his statement is inconsistent with his account (i.e. it is a Pin) suggesting, what we now know, that at this point he knew Lynsey was dead.

If someone is describing a specific historical event in the past tense ("he woke up and came downstairs") and then he/she changes one part of it ("then he would have had his breakfast, got into his car and would have driven to work"), this might suggest gaps are being filled with what 'normally' happens.

This is referred to by psychologists as using 'script memory' – general recall of what usually happens routinely. This can be used by liars to fill gaps to cover the truth. Semantic memory is often used too – this is the general knowledge we learn. It is important to ensure a person is not pressurised by questions to fill innocent memory gaps as their answers may contaminate the investigation.

We also need to ensure that we don't misjudge low levels of language skills as PIns. Baseline is key, as is the idea of clusters across channels to help with this.

Distancing

This was referred to when I mentioned a drop in volume when lying. Distancing *content* is also useful when it is introduced when referring to a certain act or person.

Examples are:

- Reduction in use of personal pronouns (e.g. 'I', 'me' and 'my'... being dropped from conversation or changing to 'it', 'we' or 'us'). There are many examples in a small but informative book by Pennebaker[49], called 'The Secret Life of Personal Pronouns' if you want to follow this up.

- Change of subject/noun terms (from 'Monica' to 'that woman'; 'my wife' to 'her').

- Weakening of emotive terms ('murdered' to 'passed away'). Mick Philpott used this latter term to describe the killing of one of the six children in the house fire that he was convicted of being involved in, and given life imprisonment for[50].

- Inappropriate concern (e.g. joking about, or making light of, a serious matter).

Now this is a good place to take a break before you look at the next topic. It is a powerful tool to add to your toolbox in getting to the truth.

Statement Analysis

We use an adapted version of CBCA (Criteria Based Content Analysis)[51]. It is derived from a system used in some USA and European courts to assess the **credibility** of child testimony in abuse cases. It is useful for you to refer to these endnotes to help you understand the origins of the criteria.[52] Our reduced and adapted criteria have not yet been approved for court use, but they have proven valuable when included in the 27 criteria for real-time veracity testing.[53]

PIns can be noted when the following criteria are found in an account from an individual as long as the account isn't led or interrupted by the questioner:

1. The account is incoherent – it is logistically impossible, e.g. puts a person at different places at the same time.

2. **Linear** (in time), overly-structured **reproduction.** When we hear rehearsed lies about past events they are often reproduced in a linear, 'train-track' format as is depicted by the red line in Figure 11. True episodes, freely recalled, tend to look more unstructured and go forward and back in time and off at tangents like the blue line. I just wish you could listen to my mother's (true) stories for great examples of the blue line! This is because memory is a reconstructive process – we rebuild stories that have happened to us from scattered parts of the brain, spontaneously, and rarely in the same sequence as the event itself.[54] Sometimes we make mistakes. This is normal forgetting and should not be confused with deception.

Figure 11: Linear, overly-structured reproduction

3. **Inappropriate detail** (in context with what we know about memory). We know from research that memory works best for events of personal or emotional significance.[55] Test this yourself by recalling where you were when you heard the tragic news of the events of '9/11' in New York. Then try to recall the activities from the day previous to that. Our (and other) research[56] has revealed that there can often be a 'shape' to detail, consistent with what we know about memory, in true (pattern 1) and false (patterns 2 and 3) accounts as illustrated in Figure 12.

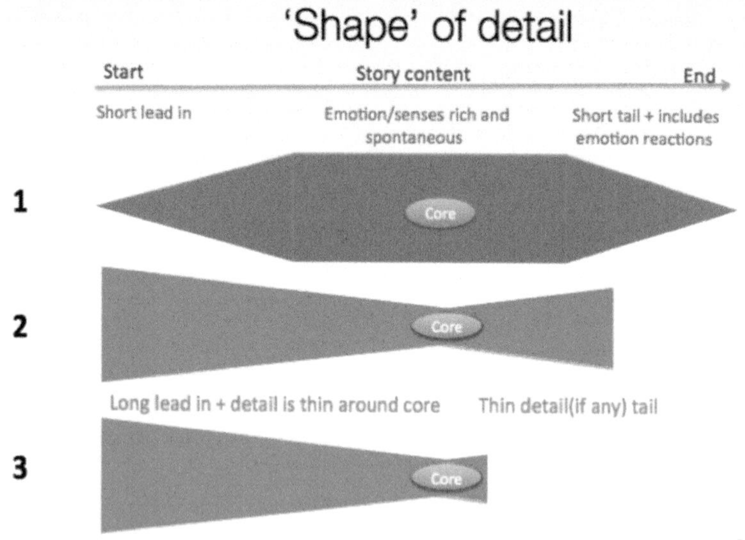

'Shape' of detail

Figure 12: Shape of detail in lies and truthful accounts

Care is needed here as I have also seen truthful accounts shaped like the third track above when the story is embarrassing and the storyteller wants to bring it to an end. So simply remember this is **only one potential Pin** (even if added to others within this section it is still **only one channel**. We need **clusters of three PIns across two channels** for us to be concerned.

4. **Lacks context.** False stories often lack the contextual detail picked up by our senses (smells, sights, sounds, tastes, temperatures, weather, etc.) as liars often forget to rehearse such detail. True statements are often peppered with these details. Lack of contextual embedding of the recalled story is a potential PIn.

5. **Lacks interactivity**. True stories will often include linked interactions between people and objects, including

paraphrased summaries or even verbatim quotations of conversations. Where these are absent, and can't be explained by the ABC, then it's a Pln.

6. **Lacks personal credibility/memory slurs** – e.g. admittance of poor memory recall, spontaneous correction of memory errors (without prompting) and self-deprecation is not really a problem. Where all such self-criticisms are lacking it may suggest the teller is in *convince* mode. It's a Pln if inconsistent with the ABC.

7. **Lacks accounts of mental states** (self and other). True stories often contain commentary about self and others, e.g.:

    1. "I was trembling as I walked through the door"

    2. "My heart started pounding when I saw her"

    3. "I was unsure about which car to buy"

    4. "He looked scared to death"

    5. "She seemed confused when I called his name"

    6. "He seemed furious as he walked into the bar".

These are often absent from stories that have been created to mislead you.

Interactive style is a big give away for liars but it is not a Pinocchio's nose. Let me stress again, we need **clusters of three Plns across two or more channels** for us to be concerned.

If we attempt to control our body language and face during a lie, the truth can often leak out from one or more of the other four channels, due to the cognitive and/or emotional load. This includes the words we use. Remember the 'truth bucket' image that I used earlier on in this book:

Figure 13: When we tell lies, we leak the truth

We only have two hands, and metaphorically speaking, even the best of us can only mask leakage from a couple of the six (channel) holes. This is an inbuilt protection into this methodology, based on innate human impulses, that happen to us in milliseconds, in a coordinated holistic way during high-stake lies - before thought has had a chance to interfere. This will prevent liars or terrorists using this information to deceive the professionals we have trained.

It was the psychoanalyst Sigmund Freud who described a variety of different types and examples of 'Freudian' or verbal slips[57].

"Almost invariably I discover a disturbing influence from something outside of the intended speech," he wrote. "The disturbing element is a single unconscious thought, which comes to light through the special blunder."

According to Freud, these errors can reveal what is going on beneath the surface – our focus, beliefs, or wishes. "Two factors seem to play a part in bringing to consciousness the substitutive names: first, the effort of attention, and second, and inner determinant which adheres to the psychic material," Freud argued. Psychology Today[58] featured an article on this phenomenon and some interesting features are extracted here for you:

> Wegner, a psychologist at Harvard, famously asked volunteers not to think of a white bear. Then he told them to speak about anything that was on their minds. In the stream of speech that followed, the forbidden white bear reared its unwanted head about once a minute... "Part of our unconscious mind is always thinking about the worst thing," explains Wegner. The unconscious thinks about worst-case scenarios to guard against them; after all, you can't prevent something from happening unless part of your brain can imagine it and check to make sure it's not actually happening. The problem is, the more the conscious mind (prefrontal cortex) wants to suppress a thought, the more the unconscious has to check to make sure we're not thinking it; so we think about it more. "We're just trying to do the right thing and not make embarrassing slips," says Wegner, "and the conscious mind usually prevails. But sometimes it fails... and the very thought we tried to suppress pops into our minds and rolls off our tongue".

When we lie the challenge is that we have to be mindful of the lie we are withholding – and at the same time we may need to fabricate an alternative story to conceal or cover the lie.

Sometimes an aspect of the truth (often a single word) may then slip into the lie. An example might be:

Be careful, though, as I have seen this in a nervous, truthful person whose first language wasn't English. My safeguard against this was that it was only one PIn, so not a concern.

Sometimes a slip can also come out as an unintended message:

"What I can tell you today is….", suggests that there may be something hidden – what can't you tell us today, and why?

This gives us clues on what we may need to verify if this slip (only a single indicator) is supported by a cluster of PIns across the channels.

Verbal Content Summary:
- Tense (C1)
- Distancing (C2)
- Statement analysis (C3)
- Verbal slip (C4)

4. Facial Expressions

Movements of one or more of the 43 muscles under the surface of the skin of the human face have proven to be very valuable indicators of emotions[59] – whether the person showing them wishes to reveal those emotions or not. This is enhanced by data from the other five channels, including Body Language and Psychophysiology, which will come next.

Thanks to Charles Darwin and Paul Ekman[60] in particular, the bulk of the scientific community accepts[61] the argument that:

1. There are universal emotions, namely, Sadness, Anger, Surprise, Happy, Fear, (albeit with some disagreement in respect to) Contempt and Disgust.

2. Facial expressions of most of these basic emotions are universal.

3. Expressions can often leak from the face as micro-expressions (less than half a second) when the owner doesn't wish to show them.

This is the basis of the five Facial Expression criteria I will cover in this section:

- FACS Anomaly (F1)

- Duration of the expression (F2)

- Symmetry across the face (F3)

- Synchrony between muscles (F4)

- Profile of the expression (F5)

FACS (Facial Action Coding System) Anomaly

We cannot see under the skin but we can see the results of the muscle activation, even tiny twitches, if we focus on the creases, bulges and furrows resulting from such movements. Not all movements are about emotion but many are. Some amateur lie detectors and entertainers use *only* facial expressions. This single channel tactic is not a reliable approach for those serious about the subject. Some researchers ignore micro facial movements (MFM) because they claim they are difficult to see. We agree it requires focus and a knowledge of the connections between the muscles and each emotion, but the value of this channel to a behaviour analyst is well worth it. There are several tools on micro-expressions around the web though I strongly recommend those developed and verified by Paul Ekman, available here for those of you who wish to test and develop your skills to see micro facial expressions - https://www.eiagroup.com/training/online-courses/

The full FACS coding system[62], developed by Paul Ekman and Wally Friesen involves around 500 different movement codes though we draw on insights from other FACS-related research[63] and will focus on FACS anomalies via only 18 key FACS codes.

These will help us to:

a) spot when an emotional display is fake or at odds with the genuine emotion being claimed, and

b) recognise a suppressed, repressed or masked emotion when it leaks as a subtle or micro-expression despite such controls.

Let's look now at the seven universal expressions of the basic emotions (Surprise, Fear, Anger, Disgust, Contempt, Sad and Happy). You may find it helpful to try to mimic some of the expressions but be careful with sadness, anger and disgust as holding these powerful expressions can start to generate the emotion within you, as the emotions and the face are hardwired, and it is a two-way street.

This emotion is very brief, one or two seconds at most when it is felt, and it often transitions into another emotion. It is triggered by something sudden and unexpected and serves to prepare us by putting the body into an attentive state. For example, the news of a surprise birthday party from your partner may bring this emotion on and, once you realise what is going on, and if you like surprise parties, this may transition into a happy emotion. Surprise often appears on the face as in Figure 14.

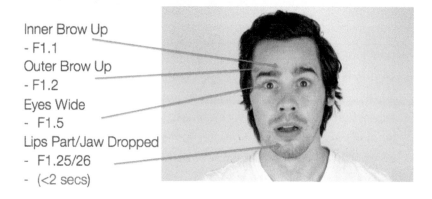

Inner Brow Up
- F1.1
Outer Brow Up
- F1.2
Eyes Wide
- F1.5
Lips Part/Jaw Dropped
- F1.25/26
- (<2 secs)

Figure 14: Surprise Facial Expression

The face is fairly relaxed and the expression is created by the activation of a cluster of muscles as indicated in the diagram. Let me explain the basics of the coding. We have codes, or our annotation shorthand, for all 27 Pins and their subsets. I have included them here and in Appendix 1 for all six channels. These face codes are drawn from the official FACS coding system used by forensic analysts and researchers.

So here in the surprise face diagram:

- 'F' tells us this is the Facial expression channel;

- The number '1' highlights that this is the first indicator (i.e. a FACS Anomaly) of the five for this channel;

- The number after the decimal point correlates with the 'FACS Action Unit' reference. The label in the diagram explains the action (e.g. F1.1 = inner brow raised).

- The note at the bottom of the diagram highlights that the reliable component to genuine surprise is that it rarely lasts for more than 2 seconds. Anything longer is probably posed as an intended, conscious signal.[64]

This expression signals to our compatriots that there is a threat of harm sensed here. Facial expressions are a long-range signalling system and can be seen from around 40 feet (13 metres) away, and we have evolved to display and see them. Figure 15 shows what it looks like.

Inner Brow Up
- F1.1
Outer Brow Up
- F1.2
Brows together
- F1.4
Eyes Wide
- F1.5
Mouth Stretch
- F1.20

Figure 15: Fear facial expression

The brows are lifted, as in surprise, though this time they are also squeezed inwards, flattening the eyebrows. This is a reliable muscle, which means it is hard to move it voluntarily. So, when we see it squeezed like this it is a reliable indicator of fear in a person. Also the mouth is stretched horizontally by a risorius muscle on each side that connects the corner of the mouth to near the hinge of the jawbone.

Fear incorporates a 'freeze' response (often before fight or flight actions). This has served our primates and animals well against being seen by predators, though this can be counter-productive in the 21st century if we freeze on a busy highway (as some rabbits do, to their peril). The term 'petrified' means fearful and the word also means 'turn to stone'. The blood travels to the main organs (heart, lungs, etc.) to help prepare us to deal with the threat, and away from the non-essential organs (digestive system and the skin) which helps explain why some lighter skinned faces pale a little when scared. More on this in channel six (Psychophysiology).

The universal trigger for anger is when someone or something interferes with our goals or compromises our principles or values. It is designed to ward of the interference and when seen can lead to the other person backing off, thereby reducing the chance of a fight. If you notice this expression emerging on your partner's face – it may be wise to back off to preserve your relationship. Here is an illustration of anger (Figure 16).

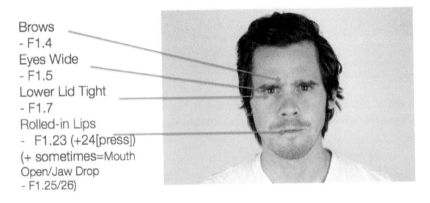

Brows
- F1.4
Eyes Wide
- F1.5
Lower Lid Tight
- F1.7
Rolled-in Lips
- F1.23 (+24[press])
(+ sometimes=Mouth
Open/Jaw Drop
- F1.25/26)

Figure 16: Anger facial expression

Here the brows are pulled together and down, sometimes angled downwards with the eyes open wide. The lower lids tighten against the eyes creating the angry 'glare' you see here. The reliable muscle is the one that rolls the red margins of the lips inwards – sometimes resulting in the lips disappearing into the mouth.

Figure 17 shows what disgust looks like.

Nose Wrinkle
- F1.9
Upper Lip Raise
- F1.10

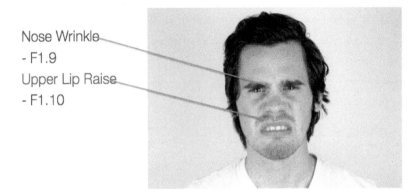

Figure 17: Disgust facial expression

The nose wrinkles and this can result in the brows being drawn down slightly. At the same time, the upper lip rises, often revealing the upper teeth if the emotion is strong. This is the reliable muscle and is hard to do unless you are feeling disgusted at something. The universal trigger is something offensive. This can be a smell, a sight or even someone using offensive language. The purpose is to try to block off the nostrils with the top lip and there is sometimes a 'yuck' sound as the throat is closed to prevent anything entering the stomach.

This describes the emotion felt when we take a position of moral superiority over another person. It's a kind of smug feeling, as, for example, when you 'look down your nose' at someone who has breached your moral code or values. Figure 18 shows two versions of this display.

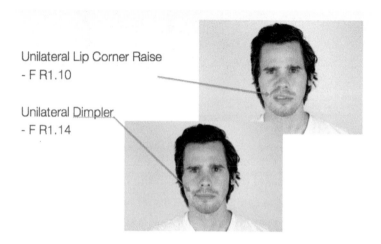

Unilateral Lip Corner Raise
- F R1.10

Unilateral Dimpler
- F R1.14

Figure 18: Contempt facial expression

Contempt is the only unilateral expression in the set – the action occurs on only one side of the face. You may notice the additional letter in the code. The letter 'R' tells us the movement of the muscle is on his right side ('L' for left). There is no research regarding which side it is displayed, and, from my experience, I have seen no patterns. Some contempt displays involve the upper lip muscle; others involve the buccinators (or cheek dimpler); some involve a combination of both. Its purpose is related to social order and has been seen flashed by an alpha male chimpanzee to a young challenger, probably indicating that 'I am in charge' which resulted in the young chimp backing off and a fight maybe prevented[65].

This emotion is often triggered by the loss of a valued person or object, and signals to others that we either need help or simply need leaving alone to recoup. Figure 19 shows it in its full expression.

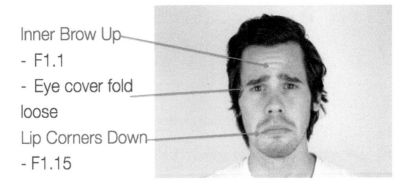

Inner Brow Up
- F1.1
- Eye cover fold
loose
Lip Corners Down
- F1.15

Figure 19: Sad facial expression

This is hard to fake as there are two sets of reliable muscles. Inner brows up are one and I have found that only around 1 in 10 people can do this as in the photo. When this is faked the eyebrows are often asymmetrical – one slightly higher than the other and squeezed together. The other reliable muscles are those pulling the lip corners downwards. When I ask people to pose sadness, they often create the downturned mouth by pushing up with the chin boss and pouting the bottom lip. Often accompanied by brows pushed downwards as in Figure 20[66].

Figure 20: Sulk expression

This 'sulk' expression is often seen in children seeking attention or attempting to get their own way.

And finally we have the happy face in Figure 21 to cheer you up after the sad face.

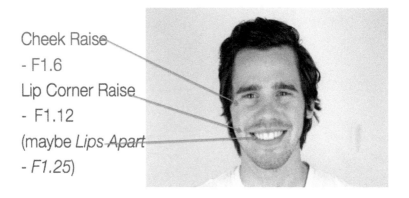

Cheek Raise
- F1.6
Lip Corner Raise
- F1.12
(maybe Lips Apart
- F1.25)

Figure 21: Happy facial expression

This may look easy but try and mimic the eyes without moving the mouth from a neutral pose – slight narrowing of the outer eyes is the result, but without you looking like you are squinting. It's not easy, as the 'doughnut-shaped' muscle around the eyes, the orbicularis oculi, is hard to contract (unless you are feeling happy) and therefore is a reliable indicator of genuine happiness. The lip corners are also pulled up towards the ears by the zygomatic major muscles. This is easy to do for most of us.

A fake, or social, smile often doesn't engage the eyes, as in Figure 22. Cover her mouth with your hand, and you will notice the eyes are not crinkling – i.e. there are no 'crow's feet' lines from the outer corners of the eyes. Be careful with this one, though, as botox and other cosmetic surgery can work against these natural effects.

Figure 22: Posed, fake or social smile

If anything, the eyes seem slightly widened, though this is hard to judge without her baseline. Her pupil dilation stands out too (maybe a dark room?, attraction?, drugs?... we don't know), though this fits under psychophysiology later, and that's just the geek in me taking over.

Duration of the Expression

We mentioned earlier that genuine surprise lasts up to a couple of seconds. Longer than that and it is probably posed as a deliberate signal, for whatever reason. Duration also features for the other emotions. Remember emotions are brief, seconds or minutes at most, and are a reaction to a trigger. When we feel something longer than this, it is often a series of the same emotion with repeating triggers. For example, you may be angered by the service from a receptionist at a hotel. You may calm down and be distracted, and then the anger emotion is triggered again every time you pass reception, visualise his/her face in your mind, or even think of the hotel or the holiday many months later. If it is longer than minutes, i.e. hours, then it could be another state such as a mood or even a disorder.

Have you ever noticed how a smile can look a little odd if it appears on a friend's face for too long? They can look weird, sinister or even a little mad! Research tells us that 'felt' pleasurable emotions produce smiles that generally last between 2/3 of a second and 4 seconds[67]. There are exceptions, though, such as micro-expressions which appear on the face for less than half a second and are often missed by the untrained. Also, expressions can be longer when the pleasure rises to full-on laughter or when we experience repeated triggers of pleasure such as looking again at an amusing image or recalling/replaying it from memory. So it is important to remember this is about pleasurable, felt emotions before any complementary, natural, follow-on reactions such as shouting, laughing, crying, fighting and running. There are many types of pleasurable emotions[68], by the way, ranging from those triggered by the senses (smell, touch, sounds, sights and tastes) to the pleasure you feel from the pride of a child's/friend's achievement. Another is *schadenfreude* – a German word with no English equivalent that is used to describe the enjoyment felt from someone else's downfall such as seeing an arrogant friend fail or trip up.

Symmetry across the face

Most expressions involve pairs of muscles across the left and right side of the face and when they are forced we often see asymmetry – one side slightly higher or lower than the other. This is especially the case on the upper face where it is argued that we have less neural connection to the forehead, brows and upper eyelids so it is hard to control them – unlike the mouth which we use for eating and speaking[69].

Some emotions engage antagonistic muscle groups, pulling face parts in opposing directions. For example, sadness often involves both an expression of sadness and the desire to control that expression. The tug-of-war across your face can result in a quivering lip.

 When facial movements are the result of felt emotions, they tend to be symmetrical. There is some good research on this[70]. Again, there are exceptions due to nerve or muscle damage, cosmetic surgery, botox, medical conditions, etc., so a baseline for each person is key. Also, we know that the emotion of 'contempt' is a unilateral expression and so is exempt here. If you can baseline a person's genuine emotions as symmetrical then any deviation with respect to symmetry is a Pin.

Synchrony across muscles

Not only do muscles generally work in symmetrical pairs, but they also work in combinations as you have seen from the seven faces of emotions. The impulse that happens within half a second of a trigger will set off the muscles in the face in most people before they are aware of the movement. In felt emotions we often see synchrony – the brows and the mouth in sadness react together. When trying to pose or fake emotions, this is very hard to do so this is another marker for fake emotions that resulted from the research (by Ekman & Frank- 1993) referred to in the last section.

Profile of the expression

Finally, let's consider the 'shape' of the onset, duration, and offset of the facial movement.

Although this varies with social context, the onset of a posed emotion is often abrupt or jagged as in this example[71].

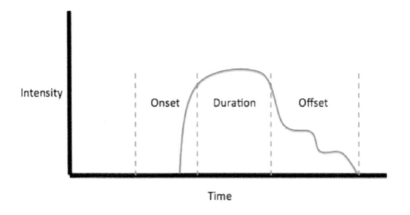

Figure 23: Fake emotion profile

A felt emotion usually has a smooth onset, short duration and smooth offset[72] as in Figure 24 unless it is disturbed by another emotion.

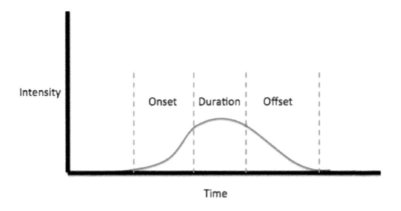

Figure 24: Profile of felt emotion

Just watch the sharp offset of the social smile often seen as a customer service staff member (e.g. air steward/ess, bus driver, hotel receptionist) turns away from an irritating customer.

This completes the criteria for the face which, to remind you, are as follows.

Facial Expression Summary:

- FACS Anomaly (F1)

- Duration of the expression (F2)

- Symmetry across the face (F3)

- Synchrony between muscles (F4)

- Profile of the expression (F5)

Let's revisit Huntley in another video where he is telling a lie to a TV reporter shortly after the girls went missing, this time outside the door of his home. We can safely assume he wants to portray concern or sadness, here, to hide any suspicion from the public that he took the girls into his house and killed them.

Pay attention to his facial expressions as he is describing 'happy, chatty girls' in VIDEO 6 in the resource site at www.gettingtothetruth.com.

You may have noticed:

1. The facial brow pose of sadness didn't match the narrative; the positive account he was offering. We saw him earlier in a police interview and this is not baseline for him and can't be explained by the sun being in his eyes. That's a FACS anomaly Pin (F1).

2. The duration is throughout this clip and the extended interview. Pin F2.

3. His brows are asymmetrical – only slightly but his right brow is higher than his left throughout. The extra creasing above his right brow accentuates this difference. Pin F3.

4. In felt sadness we see synchrony between the reliable muscles of the mouth and brows. No engagement of the sad muscles in the mouth is evident. Pin (F4).

5. No onset or offset – this is a fixed, held display that doesn't follow what we know about emotional profiles. Pin (F5).

Five Pins in eight seconds. However, we still need another channel to corroborate the lie. Luckily, here it comes in the body language section, where I will revisit this video.

5. Body Language

Although we have universal facial expressions of emotions, we have not yet discovered a universal signal from the body that has the same meaning across all cultures and generations. This takes us back to the critical factor of **baseline**. We need to understand what each person normally means by the gesture we see (if anything), not what it means to us. Even if we are from the same country and belief system. This is the most widely written about channel and many of the theories offered are contradictory so I have distilled the channel down to what is known to be reliable.

Here, then, are the five reliable criteria relating to Body Language:

- Gestural slip (B1)

- Illustrators (B2)

- Manipulators (B3)

- Tension (B4)

- Eyes (B5)

Gestural slip

A gesture is an emblem or a signal made by the hands or body that signals meaning without the need for words.

Can you think of a few common gestures that are used between you and friends?

Examples might include the following:

1. Thumb up

2. Thumb down

3. Circle formed with thumb and forefinger

4. Middle finger pointing up, nail away from you

5. First two fingers pointing up, nails away from you

6. Head nod up and down

7. Head shake side to side

8. Shoulders shrug upwards

9. One outer eyebrow lifted

10. Both eyebrows lifted.

These last two are included to remind you that every movement on the face isn't an automatic emotional display. Some can indicate cognitive load or confusion. Some are signals, or emblems, we consciously make to others when interacting. For example, a raising of the eyebrows may be an invitation for another to speak.

Many gestures are made by the hands. Thumb up, for example, can mean many things:

- it can indicate that things are ok

- in scuba diving, it can be a statement that you are surfacing

- in some cultures, it is rude and offensive.

A signal made by moving the head up and down can:

- signal agreement or 'yes' to many people in the UK and USA

- signal disagreement or 'no' to many others (especially if accompanied with an eye closure, and maybe a 'tut' sound in Turkey or Romania).

In parts of India there are many common gestures using the head – each with their own meaning. Search for these on *YouTube* if you are interested.

Most gestures are meant to be seen and are therefore quite big signals of the body, head, shoulders or face, or made with the fingers and hands in a presentation zone which is about the size of a beachball held out in front of our chest. The gestural slip PIn is noted when the gesture isn't consistent with what the person is attempting to convey to you and it is only worthy of note if it is leakage.

Leakage is often below the consciousness of the sender and can be:

1. A gesture, usually with the hands, that appears outside the presentation zone

2. A micro-gesture. A tiny fragment of a gesture (one-centimetre movement or less is a guide – larger than this, and it is probably a deliberate signal).

A popular example of the first one can be seen when Senator Obama was speaking about political opponents and at the same time scratches his cheek with his middle finger. (Google search

'Obama McCain flipping the bird' and you will find one of a few examples). Is he mischievously doing this with knowledge? Or might he be unconscious of the strong feelings the then Senator was feeling towards Senator McCain? I don't know.

The second type of leakage, micro-gesture, is very commonly seen in our work, especially when it is the fragment of a head nod or a head shake that contradicts a negative/affirmative statement from a person. Remember cultural and individual differences, and find out what they do with their head when they say 'yes' and 'no' first (i.e. their baseline).

One micro-gesture that also occurs within many countries I have visited is a shoulder shrug. When displayed fully, such a shrug can be used to signal 'don't know' or 'not sure' (i.e., uncertainty). I have found, though, that some of my Japanese clients don't recognise this meaning, from this gesture - so more research is needed to see how universal this interpretation is. This shrug can appear in several parts of the body:

- Single-sided micro shoulder shrug upwards

- Double-sided micro shoulder shrug

- Single-sided micro hand shrug (rotates outward)

- Double-sided micro hand shrug

- Mouth shrug (arched down lips created by pushing up the chin boss)

- A combination of some of the above.

So if a person is saying something positive and confidently, whilst contradicting it with a single sided micro-gesture, then this is a PIn. If you want to see one let's return to Ian Huntley's interview

(VIDEO 1 at www.gettingtothetruth.com) and watch his right shoulder when he is speaking with confidence to try to convince the police he was innocent when he replies, 'Physical contact?...No'

Even with his right arm tightly clamped by his left, maybe to prevent leakage, he can't stop the micro-right-shoulder-shrug that contradicts his reply. This is leakage. A clash with his 'account' and therefore a PIn. It accompanies the other eleven PIns across three channels making this a huge red-flag from just three words. The police officer has highlighted the truth with a good, unexpected, probing question – it is highly likely that he had physical contact with them in order to kill them. Soon after this episode Huntley closes down, unable to sustain his lie, and later confesses to the crime.

Illustrators

These are movements, usually of the hands (though can include face and body movements), that accompany speech to reinforce or emphasize what we wish to say. The two things that help us make our truth and lie decisions are to do with:

- Change in use – increases and decreases which cannot be explained by the Account, Baseline or Context and/or

- Illustrators that aren't split-second synchronised with the point being vocalised.

The first issue might highlight cognitive or emotional load. The second can suggest that this may be a performance, rather than full ownership of a message being spoken.

Manipulators

These describe those actions when one body part touches or fiddles with another body part. Or it could be that someone fiddles with an object like a pen, button, hair-strands or jewellery. This can be due to relaxation or nervousness and is of limited use in behaviour analysis unless we see increases and decreases which cannot be explained by the Account, Baseline or Context. Only then is the manipulator a PIn.

Tension

Muscle tension (face/hands/arms/torso/legs) can occur when we are stressed or fearful and needs to be looked at to determine whether it fits with what is going on. Tension out of context could be:

- Reactive - signalling anxiety, fear (body back), anger or stress as a result of what is going on, or it could be

- Proactive – deliberate attempts to convince (body forward), or tension to suppress or prevent leakage from the face or body when someone is trying to hide inner thoughts or feelings.

Either way, changes in muscle tension is a Pin if the behaviour can't be explained by the ABC.

First of all, let's define the difference. Eye closure is defined under Paul Ekman's Facial Action Coding System as being *eyes closed for half a second or more*. This is a useful marker that can highlight when an individual may be distancing themselves from what they are saying, in a similar way to when the voice volume drops or personal pronouns reduce in frequency. Eye blinking can be helpful too, though, like eye closure, this is only one PIn (when not accounted for by ABC), and thus needs linking to the type of activity in which the 'blinker' is engaged. Unless a person is suffering dust, air-conditioning, wearing contact lenses or has had eye surgery, or suffers a condition of the eyes (e.g. Glaucoma), then their eyeball only needs one blink every 12-15 seconds to lubricate it – around 4 or 5 blinks per minute.

This changes if that person is:

1. Reading – blinking decreases to scan the words

2. Listening – baseline or slowed or stalled blink rate if they need to work hard to absorb or organize what they are hearing

3. Speaking – a slight increase in truthful speech as they recall their story or present their account

4. Thinking hard – blinking decreases or stops with cognitive load

5. Convincing/lying – blinking decreases as they stare at you to convince you, or check if they are being believed.

6. Recovering from a stare – blinking increases to lubricate the dry eyes created by point 4 and 5.

We often see a pattern when people lie that is a succession of some of these phases. Blinking stops as they construct the lie...they then stare through the lie...then a few blinks to recover. Research supports this[73].

So to summarise:

Body Language Summary:
- Gestural slip (B1)
- Illustrators (B2)
- Manipulators (B3)
- Tension (B4)
- Eyes (B5)

6. Psychophysiology

Finally, we have the reactions within the body that stem from chemical and electrical changes affecting the major organs. While these biometric indicators of what the Autonomic Nervous System (ANS) is doing often need technical equipment and biometric sensors to pick them up, there are many clues from behaviour and appearance that can point to these changes.

Let's first lay out the Psychophysiology criteria:

- Heart rate (P1)

- Perspiration (P2)

- Temperature (P3)

- Blood pressure (P4)

- Breathing (P5)

- Digestion (P6)

- Pupils (P7).

Recent technological innovations and advances mean that it should be possible to incorporate tools, within behaviour analysis work, which provide ANS information beyond the physiological signals which can be humanly seen/heard.

I recognize that most of these measure stress or anxiety though we are currently experimenting with data collection tools that can be fed into a 'hypothesizing-human-decision-maker' including:

- thermal cameras to help users to 'see' local blood circulation in others

- laser-Doppler-vibrometers that can measure blood pressure and heart rate from 50 meters away from the subject (used in military triage in enemy territory)

- pixel movement/colour changes (amplified by a factor of a hundred) so that users can pick up skin colour changes and movement/micro-expressions that the naked eye may not (including, a pulse)

- multichannel polygraph equipment

- 'Kinect' type technology – used in computer gaming - to pick up the slightest body movement

- remote pupilometry which is making advances into indexes of cognitive/emotional activity and load.

The above bring challenges, as well as potential benefits. Overt technology can create behavioural changes which contaminate evaluations, as we know from the criticisms around the field of polygraphy (National Research Council, 2003). The ethics and practicalities of using covert equipment can complicate, rather than aid, real-world analysis.

In addition, if/when it becomes possible for users to have access to the data picked up by such tools during *real-time* (as opposed to *post-event*) analysis, we will need to consider whether simultaneous data-overload might lead to a deterioration of performance in users' real-time assessments across the six channels. This needs more research.

A related issue is achieving buy-in from professionals (working in high-stakes contexts) who have limited time and capacity to capture simultaneous, multimodal data from a human; especially when they are working alone. With challenging base-rates (large volumes of innocent people compared to the low volume of people with mal-intent) and long working shifts, we are coaching staff to 'reset' their attention for every person with full attentiveness. Staff may also be restricted (by ethics, protocols, legislation, etc.) from using covert or overt technology. This includes police, military personnel, security professionals, HR screeners, recruiters, negotiators, medics, purchasers, social workers, and so on.

All is not lost with biometrics, however, especially when we look at what our natural senses can detect:

1. Some people have prominent carotid arteries or veins on their temples or centre forehead which can highlight increases in blood pressure. I know... this sounds geeky, but just watch actress Julia Roberts' centre forehead vein when she really gets into her character role and becomes stressed, angry or fearful in her movie roles. Of course, like other data in this channel, we need to work out which of these she is feeling and check it against the ABC before we can mark it as one of the PIns in the cluster.

2. The stress-response fight(anger) or flight(fear) states can also cause the digestion system to cease as the sympathetic nervous system kicks in. This response brigades resources towards the other essential organs (heart/lungs/muscles) as the body is primed to respond to whatever triggered those states. The digestion system isn't needed in these moments, and thus the stomach and salivation functions wind down, often leaving the mouth dry. The clues that this is happening are in the increased swallowing, lip-licking, and water-sipping, as seen from nervous public speakers and liars. If inconsistent with the ABC... it's a Pln.

3. Perspiration can be seen as a change in the glow on a forehead or the change in dampness in a hand-shake before during and after an interview. Take care again, here, as warm rooms, flu, anxiety, fear of being disbelieved, and deception are all possible, and these need testing with good probes.

4. Breathing rate changes are quite easy to see and the stopping of breathing is common in fear, with shorter breaths in the upper chest being a possible signal of anger or fear. If the change is out of context, then this is a Pln.

5. Warm faces can signal anger; cold faces can signal fear. In some skin tones this can be seen as a skin colour change. This is caused by changes in local blood flow away or towards the extremities, ears, nose and the skin surface.

6. Pupil size is affected by cognitive and emotional load though this is a complex area and very hard to monitor in conditions where lighting isn't constant. We also need to

consider that the person of interest may be under the influence of drugs or medicines and it can be very difficult to see changes with those people who have a dark brown iris. I include it on the PIns list, though, since pupil dilation and contraction is very difficult to consciously control by liars. I feel pupils will play an increasing role in the data-mix as biometric measures on webcams, and in airports and security contexts, move forward.

Psychophysiology summary:

- Heart rate (P1)
- Perspiration (P2)
- Temperature (P3)
- Blood pressure (P4)
- Breathing (P5)
- Digestion (P6)
- Pupils (P7).

Before I wrap up this section, you may wish to review a 13-second clip from an example of another video I have consulted on. This is Stuart Hazel, partner of Tia Sharp's grandmother who was staying in their home. Six days before this news interview Tia was reported as missing, and Hazel was asked to help with an interview to appeal to the public for help in finding her. Hazel was the last to see her alive and reported that Tia had left the house, alive and well, to go into a local town.

See what physiological (and other) indicators you can notice from the short clip labelled VIDEO 7 at www.gettingtothetruth.com.

Make notes about what you hear and see before you move on to see what I highlighted to the client.

You may have noticed:

Secs	Account / Utterance (stress)	PIns	Hypothesis 1 (truth teller – true appeal)	Hypothesis 2 (involved in disappearance)
0-2	"I want to be out there looking in the fields…"	F1/2/3/4/5 - Inner brows squeezed and raised throughout 13 secs (and whole interview) – long duration. Mouth neutral. Slight asymmetry (left brow raise stronger). V3 - Voice strong. V5 – verbal slip.	Anxiety of TV overriding genuine emotion?	Feigning sadness/ concern? Admitting knowledge that she is no longer alive and this was his plan?
2-3	"…don't wanna find her in a field".	F1 - Brows down, then squared and squeezed with widened eyes.	Realisation that she could be dead?	Cognitive load realising he has just suggested that she is dead followed by fear? ("What have I just said!!")

3-7	(Pause …)	P5/5 - 2 short breaths out. B1 - Slight head shake 'no'.	Thought of her being dead?	Self-control? "'Oh no!"
7-10	"I wanna find her sitting in the bloody Mc**Don alds** sitting there spendin g my **tenner**".	P7 - Blink rate decreases. V1 - Volume increase. V3 - Tone (change in voice quality). S2 - Lightening the atmosphere.	Hoping for a good outcome to missing Tia?	Lying? Trying to recover situation?
10-13	(Pause …)	P6/6 - 2 lip licks. B1 - Look away. P5 - Short breath out. S3 - Slight laughter.	Anxiety at being on TV?	Emotional (fearful) reaction to his error?

The truth is that throughout this interview the body of Tia was hidden above their heads in the attic. Hazell was found guilty of Tia's murder and is serving life-imprisonment for his crime.

PART THREE – Into Practice

We have now learned to recognise behavioural indicators, or PIns, that reveal something else is probably going on behind a statement being made by others.

The challenge is that:

We may see or hear something,

but we don't know 'why'.

This is why good probes or elicitation techniques are needed, whether you are engaged in a casual conversation with a purpose, or a more formal interview scenario.

The secret weapon for the truth seeker is 'surprise'. The aim is to provide a series of unexpected stimuli that are no problem for a truth teller, yet pose a potential problem for the liar.

This is often in the form of an unexpected question. It can also be a sniffer dog at the airport, a uniformed security officer early in the queue leading into a large public/sports event or security cameras and scanner equipment. We are interested in the behavioural reaction to strategically created and positioned stimuli, so that we can channel our efforts and organisational resources on those with mal-intent while not restricting, scaring and annoying the innocent.

So, to make more accurate judgments of deception, truth/lie-catchers must aim to take an active role using probes or questions to help them to generate behavioural differences between liars and truth-tellers[74]. I call these probes, 'amplifiers', as they can serve to explore, test or verify something you think you have noticed around the core of the story another person is offering to you.

There are situations in challenging real-life situations where we aren't authorised to 'interview' someone (e.g. when working undercover or where the perception of you carrying out 'an interview' is inappropriate or may be resisted). Also, we may only have a few minutes, sometimes less than a minute – maybe only one chance to get to the truth or to assess risk (e.g. security, police, negotiations and suspected unfaithful partners). There are advanced elicitation techniques that we cover in our live courses (https://www.eiagroup.com/training/live-courses/) that benefit from face-to-face practice. However, here is a practical approach of how to approach your interactions and interviews with others.

Whether it's a negotiation with someone selling a car to you or a more formal interview or negotiation as part of your profession, it is valuable to have a plan.

The secret with questions is to have a framework, while maintaining flexibility.

Some professions have their own models to fit local protocols and legislation, and readers are encouraged to check those out – whether they be good or bad – as there will be reasons for them. In the absence of a model, I offer you a generic framework here that has been influenced by a number of disciplines, as well as scientific research. It follows the acronym, 'PEEVR'[75].

It is a versatile framework that allows for changes, adaptations, and tailoring and you are encouraged to use this as a default model to reflect on and develop your own approach.

PEEVR Model

PEEVR represents:

- **P**lanning and Preparation

- **E**ngagement

- **E**xploration

- **V**erification

- **R**esolution.

Whilst this is a dynamic model that needs to respond to the context and adapt to what emerges between the parties, there is a general flow through the framework.

So let's start with Planning and Preparation.

This is primarily about what happens **before** engaging others in conversations or interviews though re-planning, time-outs and further research may be necessary to enable success once you are further into the model.

Planning and Preparation - Considerations and Tips:

- **Role** - Is it your job/duty to even get involved in this?

- **Homework** - In many cases you need to do your research on the **case** (history/intelligence/facts) and the **person** (life experiences, preferences, gender, age, beliefs, values, culture, language, personality, attitudes, health, relationships, hobbies, idiosyncrasies, fears, goals, etc).

- **Or not** - In other cases it may be better to take them 'at face value' without any prior contamination.

- **Macro context** – the backdrop to this situation (major events, political, social, economic, technological, environmental, legal, etc.)

- **Micro context** - At this **time** ...to respect preferences and rituals (hour/day/month)? In this **place** (location/setting)? Layout (formal/ informal/power influences/desks/ chairs/lighting)?

- **Self-check** – Are you in the right state (emotion/stress/health/ tiredness/preoccupations/hunger/cravings) to have this conversation? Relax, be mindful and achieve an attentive state conducive to the purpose of collecting multi-channel data.

- **Objectivity** – Are you aware of your biases (we all have them)? Are you using your perspective to evaluate others (e.g. "I wouldn't do that" – a bias I call 'ME Theory')? Have you already judged the other(s)? Can you manage these biases?

- **Their position** – Have you considered this from their perspective?

- **Roles and responsibilities** – Who needs to be involved? Alone or a team? Who does what?

- **Technology/Records** – notes, audio/video recording?

- **Other protocols** – Legalities, policies, permissions, procedures, ethics?

Engagement

Is about the psychological 'handshake' where the aim is often to secure trust and achieve rapport between you and the other(s) and to get their full account or story – to encourage them to share what they are willing and able to share with you relating to the purpose of the conversation. The key is having a mindset towards curiosity, seeking first to fully understand the other(s), not to judge them.

Engagement - Considerations and Tips:

- **First impressions** – What you do in the first few seconds of meeting another will set the tone for the conversation. Get curious, be interested. Get in an attentive state.

- **Introductions** – meet and greet, exchange and use names.

- **Baseline** – generate conversation from the other that uses content you can corroborate as true. Start to gather baseline behaviour across the six channels (voice, face, body, interactional style, verbal content, psychophysiology) during these chats in the context where, later, you may wish to dig deeper in a non-accusatory way. Try to keep the context **constant** so changes in baseline can be classified as PIns... not changes in context.

- **Purpose** – establish it and check it is shared/understood.

- **Contract in** – for honesty both ways. Request as much detail as possible. Say it is ok if you can't remember something.

- **Permission** – does it need securing to have the conversation? For how long can we have this meeting? Is another place/time going to be more constructive? Rights and ethics?

- **Professionalism and competence** – needs to be fit for the purpose of the conversation. In a crime-suspect scenario they need to know that if they are innocent and truthful they are safe as you are best qualified to make sure they don't get wrongly accused. However, if they are guilty then the truth is the best approach so we can help them to move forward.

- **Account** – Get their story without leading or contaminating it with your words, manner or approaches. Tell me…? Please explain…? Can you describe…..? The account is what the person wants to share with you about a **past** history/episode they claim to have experienced, their **current** knowledge/position/identity/opinion or their **future** plans and intentions.

- **Account+** - Anything else? And? Mm..mm? and other 'encouragers' to exhaust the story.

- **Summarise back** – key points, using their words, to clarify and show that you have been attentive.

Exploration

Once the account is exhausted you may wish to explore the account a little deeper if it is your role to do so. This may be to help a child, friend, neighbour, colleague or partner to talk something through when it is troubling them. Or it may be to enter discovery mode, where you feel there is something that isn't being shared that needs to be.

In many cases it might be none of your business and you should just leave it alone. Having these skills does not give you the right to become a self-appointed counsellor, detective, or irritating pest.

If, however, you notice a cluster of PIns, where the stakes are high (and the consequences of missing the truth could be damaging to you, the other person, or a third party you care about) then explore away!

Exploration - Considerations and Tips:

- **Hypotheses testing** – collect data, consider alternatives – suspend judgment and bias.

- **Targeted questioning** – concentrate on the 'core issues' and the PIns around them. Explore what the other was/is thinking and feeling around those key issues.

Verification

This is where you can cross-check and verify what you are hearing and seeing. You may need to revisit a problem area where you have seen Pins with a question that you should try to pose in a non-accusatory way to check if you have:

- coherence throughout the story

- consistency across the channels

- spontaneity and natural flow

- appropriate detail to fit with the story

- interactions

- contextual embedding

- and all the other factors associated with memory[76] when people recall their stories to you.

If there is consistency across the six channels, with the story (account), with the baseline of the individual, and it fits the macro and micro context, then you have most likely found the truth. Avoid interrogating until you find a Pin... a common error.

If you do have Pins, that cannot be explained by the ABC's, then keep working if the truth is important.

Verification - Considerations and Tips:

- **Re-runs** – ask the other to tell you again about the core of the story or the section where you have seen/heard many Pins.

- **Multi-level questioning** – use appropriate 'levels of questions' and don't stay just with words and the detail. Look deeper into the meaning behind those words, and the thoughts and feelings that you are now trained to read. Establish the values and beliefs that may be driving the behaviour, actions and communication from others.

At some point you may need to make a decision.

- Do you buy the used car?

- Do you appoint the job applicant?

- Do you arrest the suspect?

- Do you accept the claim of the politician?

- Do you keep your shares in 'Company X' having heard the CEOs projections for the next 12 months?

- Do you stay in the relationship after a suspected affair by your partner?

- Do you accept your teenager's denial regarding where he/she was last night?

Or, do you choose to **not make a decision,** so you can loop back into the PEEVR framework, to verify the facts, with corroboration from elsewhere, as needed.

Afterword

Always remember – does it really matter? And is it your role or duty to intervene?

I would like to finish by going back to the ethical point made at the start of Part Two of this book.

With power comes responsibility. These insights into behaviour will give you information that others may not have intended for you to have. You may not be able to turn off what you see and hear, though you are able to suspend what you do with such insight.

So unless the stakes are high, or it is your professional role to get to the truth, please remember that:

It is healthier to believe and trust in others,
and occasionally be let down, rather than live a life of distrust
and distance yourself from those you care about.

Appendix I – SCAnR Coding Summary

EIA SCAnR Criteria (with coding references in brackets):

Interactional Style:

- Flow (S1)

- Evasiveness (S2)

- Impression management (S3)

Voice:

- Volume (V1)

- Pitch (V2)

- Tone (V3)

Verbal Content:

- Tense (C1)

- Distancing (C2)

- Statement analysis (C3)

- Verbal slip (C4)

Facial Expression:

- FACS Anomaly (F1)

- Duration of the expression (F2)

- Symmetry across the face (F3)

- Synchrony between muscles (F4)

- Profile of the expression (F5)

Body Language:

- Gestural slip (B1)

- Illustrators (B2)

- Manipulators (B3)

- Tension (B4)

- Eyes (B5)

Psychophysiology:

- Heart rate (P1)

- Perspiration (P2)

- Temperature (P3)

- Blood pressure (P4)

- Breathing (P5)

- Digestion (P6)

- Pupils (P7).

Appendix II – Research behind the 27 Criteria

Interactional Style :

1. Flow

ANOLLI, L. and CICERI, R., 1997. The voice of deception: Vocal strategies of naive and able liars. Journal of Nonverbal Behaviour, 21(4), pp. 259-284.

ARCIULI, J., MALLARD, D. and VILLAR, G., 2010. "Um, I can tell you're lying": Linguistic markers of deception versus truth-telling in speech. Applied Psycholinguistics, 31(03), pp. 397-411.

BACHOROWSKI, J. and OWREN, M.J., 1995. Vocal expression of emotion: Acoustic properties of speech are associated with emotional intensity and context. Psychological Science, 6(4), pp. 219-224.

DEPAULO, B.M., LINDSAY, J.J., MALONE, B.E., MUHLENBRUCK, L., CHARLTON, K. and COOPER, H., 2003. Cues to deception. Psychological bulletin, 129(1), pp. 74.

EKMAN, P., 2009. Telling Lies: Clues to Deceit in the Marketplace, Politics, and Marriage (Revised Edition). WW Norton & Company.

HIRSCHBERG, J.B., BENUS, S., ENOS, F. and SHRIBERG, E., 2006. Pauses in Deceptive Speech, 2006, Proc. ISCA 3rd International Conference on Speech Prosody

HUMPHERYS, S.L., 2010. A system of deception and fraud detection using reliable linguistic cues including hedging, disfluencies, and repeated phrases.

JUSLIN, P.N. and LAUKKA, P., 2003. Communication of emotions in vocal expression and music performance: Different channels, same code? Psychological bulletin, 129(5), pp. 770.

LAUKKA, P., JUSLIN, P. and BRESIN, R., 2005. A dimensional approach to vocal expression of emotion. Cognition & Emotion, 19(5), pp. 633-653.

MANN, S., VRIJ, A. and BULL, R., 2002. Suspects, lies, and videotape: An analysis of authentic high-stake liars. Law and human behaviour, 26(3), pp. 365-376.

PORTER, S. and BRINKE, L., 2010. The truth about lies: What works in detecting high-stakes deception? Legal and Criminological Psychology, 15(1), pp. 57-75.

ROCKWELL, P., BULLER, D.B. and BURGOON, J.K., 1997. The voice of deceit: Refining and expanding vocal cues to deception. Communication Research Reports, 14(4), pp. 451-459.

TEN BRINKE, L., MACDONALD, S., PORTER, S. and O'CONNOR, B., 2012. Crocodile tears: Facial, verbal and body language behaviours associated with genuine and fabricated remorse. Law and human behaviour, 36(1), pp. 51.

VERNHAM, Z., VRIJ, A., LEAL, S., MANN, S. and HILLMAN, J., 2014. Collective interviewing: A transactive memory approach towards identifying signs of truthfulness. Journal of Applied Research in Memory and Cognition, 3(1), pp. 12-20.

VRIJ, A., EDWARD, K., ROBERTS, K.P. and BULL, R., 2000. Detecting deceit via analysis of verbal and nonverbal behaviour. Journal of Nonverbal Behaviour, 24(4), pp. 239-263.

VRIJ, A. and HEAVEN, S., 1999. Vocal and verbal indicators of deception as a function of lie complexity. Psychology, crime and law, 5(3), pp. 203-215.

YILDIRIM, S., BULUT, M., LEE, C.M., KAZEMZADEH, A., DENG, Z., LEE, S., NARAYANAN, S. and BUSSO, C., 2004. An acoustic study of emotions expressed in speech. INTERSPEECH 2004.

ZUCKERMAN, M., DEPAULO, B.M. and ROSENTHAL, R., 1981. Verbal and nonverbal communication of deception. Advances in experimental social psychology, 14, pp. 1-59.

2. Evasiveness

CARPENTER, R.H., 1981. Stylistic analysis for law enforcement purposes: A case study of a language variable as an index of a suspect's caution in phrasing answers. Communication Quarterly, 29(1), pp. 32-39.

CHOUDHURY, F., 2014. CAN LANGUAGE BE USEFUL IN DETECTING DECEPTION? THE LINGUISTIC MARKERS OF DECEPTION IN THE JODI ARIAS INTERVIEW. Diffusion-The UCLan Journal of Undergraduate Research, 7(2),.

DRISKELL, J.E., SALAS, E. and DRISKELL, T., 2012. Social indicators of deception. Human factors, 54(4), pp. 577-588.

COLWELL, K., HISCOCK, C.K. and MEMON, A., 2002. Interviewing techniques and the assessment of statement credibility. Applied Cognitive Psychology, 16(3), pp. 287-300.

COLWELL, K., HISCOCK-ANISMAN, C.K., MEMON, A., TAYLOR, L. and PREWETT, J., 2007. Assessment Criteria Indicative of Deception (ACID): An integrated system of investigative interviewing and detecting deception. Journal of Investigative Psychology and Offender Profiling, 4(3), pp. 167-180.

HUMPHERYS, S.L., 2010. A system of deception and fraud detection using reliable linguistic cues including hedging, disfluencies, and repeated phrases.

PORTER, S. and BRINKE, L., 2010. The truth about lies: What works in detecting high-stakes deception? Legal and Criminological Psychology, 15(1), pp. 57-75.

3. Impression management

CARPENTER, R.H., 1981. Stylistic analysis for law enforcement purposes: A case study of a language variable as an index of a suspect's caution in phrasing answers. Communication Quarterly,

29(1), pp. 32-39.

CHOUDHURY, F., 2014. CAN LANGUAGE BE USEFUL IN DETECTING DECEPTION? THE LINGUISTIC MARKERS OF DECEPTION IN THE JODI ARIAS INTERVIEW. Diffusion-The UCLan Journal of Undergraduate Research, 7(2),.

DRISKELL, J.E., SALAS, E. and DRISKELL, T., 2012. Social indicators of deception. Human factors, 54(4), pp. 577-588.

COLWELL, K., HISCOCK, C.K. and MEMON, A., 2002. Interviewing techniques and the assessment of statement credibility. Applied Cognitive Psychology, 16(3), pp. 287-300.

COLWELL, K., HISCOCK-ANISMAN, C.K., MEMON, A., TAYLOR, L. and PREWETT, J., 2007. Assessment Criteria Indicative of Deception (ACID): An integrated system of investigative interviewing and detecting deception. Journal of Investigative Psychology and Offender Profiling, 4(3), pp. 167-180.

IRELAND, M.E., SLATCHER, R.B., EASTWICK, P.W., SCISSORS, L.E., FINKEL, E.J. and PENNEBAKER, J.W., 2011. Language style matching predicts relationship initiation and stability. Psychological science, 22(1), pp. 39-44.

PORTER, S. and BRINKE, L., 2010. The truth about lies: What works in detecting high-stakes deception? Legal and Criminological Psychology, 15(1), pp. 57-75.

VERNHAM, Z., VRIJ, A., LEAL, S., MANN, S. and HILLMAN, J., 2014. Collective interviewing: A transactive memory approach towards identifying signs of truthfulness. Journal of Applied Research in Memory and Cognition, 3(1), pp. 12-20.

WHITE, C.H. and BURGOON, J.K., 2001. Adaptation and communicative design. Human Communication Research, 27(1), pp. 9-37.

Voice :

4. Volume

BACHOROWSKI, J. and OWREN, M.J., 1995. Vocal expression of emotion: Acoustic properties of speech are associated with emotional intensity and context. Psychological Science, 6(4), pp. 219-224.

EKMAN, P., 2009. Telling Lies: Clues to Deceit in the Marketplace, Politics, and Marriage (Revised Edition). WW Norton & Company.

EKMAN, P., 2007. Emotions revealed: Recognizing faces and feelings to improve communication and emotional life. Macmillan.

FRICK, R.W., 1985. Communicating emotion: The role of prosodic features. Psychological bulletin, 97(3), pp. 412.

HOLLIEN, H.F., 1990. The acoustics of crime. Springer Science & Business Media.

ROCKWELL, P., BULLER, D.B. and BURGOON, J.K., 1997. The voice of deceit: Refining and expanding vocal cues to deception. Communication Research Reports, 14(4), pp. 451-459.

5. Pitch

ANOLLI, L. and CICERI, R., 1997. The voice of deception: Vocal strategies of naive and able liars. Journal of Nonverbal Behaviour, 21(4), pp. 259-284.

BACHOROWSKI, J. and OWREN, M.J., 1995. Vocal expression of emotion: Acoustic properties of speech are associated with emotional intensity and context. Psychological Science, 6(4), pp. 219-224.

DEPAULO, B.M., STONE, J.I. and LASSITER, G.D., 1985. Deceiving and detecting deceit. The self and social life, 323.

EKMAN, P., FRIESEN, W.V. and SCHERER, K.R., 1976. Body

movement and voice pitch in deceptive interaction. *Semiotica*, 16(1), pp. 23-28.

EKMAN, P., 2009. *Telling Lies: Clues to Deceit in the Marketplace, Politics, and Marriage (Revised Edition)*. WW Norton & Company.

EKMAN, P., 2007. *Emotions revealed: Recognizing faces and feelings to improve communication and emotional life*. Macmillan.

ELFENBEIN, H.A. and AMBADY, N., 2002. On the universality and cultural specificity of emotion recognition: a meta-analysis. *Psychological bulletin*, 128(2), pp. 203.

FRICK, R.W., 1985. Communicating emotion: The role of prosodic features. *Psychological bulletin*, 97(3), pp. 412.

HOLLIEN, H.F., 1990. *The acoustics of crime*. Springer Science & Business Media.

JUSLIN, P.N. and LAUKKA, P., 2003. Communication of emotions in vocal expression and music performance: Different channels, same code? *Psychological bulletin*, 129(5), pp. 770.

LAUKKA, P., JUSLIN, P. and BRESIN, R., 2005. A dimensional approach to vocal expression of emotion. *Cognition & Emotion*, 19(5), pp. 633-653.

LAUKKA, P., JUSLIN, P. and BRESIN, R., 2005. A dimensional approach to vocal expression of emotion. *Cognition & Emotion*, 19(5), pp. 633-653.

ROCKWELL, P., BULLER, D.B. and BURGOON, J.K., 1997. The voice of deceit: Refining and expanding vocal cues to deception. *Communication Research Reports*, 14(4), pp. 451-459.

SCHERER, K.R., 1986. Voice, stress, and emotion. *Dynamics of stress*. Springer, pp. 157-179.

STREETER, L.A., KRAUSS, R.M., GELLER, V., OLSON, C. and APPLE, W., 1977. Pitch changes during attempted deception. *Journal of personality and social psychology*, 35(5), pp. 345.

VERVERIDIS, D. and KOTROPOULOS, C., 2006. Emotional speech recognition: Resources, features, and methods. *Speech*

Communication, 48(9), pp. 1162-1181.

YILDIRIM, S., BULUT, M., LEE, C.M., KAZEMZADEH, A., DENG, Z., LEE, S., NARAYANAN, S. and BUSSO, C., 2004. An acoustic study of emotions expressed in speech. INTERSPEECH 2004.

ZUCKERMAN, M., DEPAULO, B.M. and ROSENTHAL, R., 1981. Verbal and nonverbal communication of deception. Advances in experimental social psychology, 14, pp. 1-59.

6. Tone

BACHOROWSKI, J. and OWREN, M.J., 1995. Vocal expression of emotion: Acoustic properties of speech are associated with emotional intensity and context. Psychological Science, 6(4), pp. 219-224.

EKMAN, P., 2009. Telling Lies: Clues to Deceit in the Marketplace, Politics, and Marriage (Revised Edition). WW Norton & Company.

EKMAN, P., 2007. Emotions revealed: Recognizing faces and feelings to improve communication and emotional life. Macmillan.

FRICK, R.W., 1985. Communicating emotion: The role of prosodic features. Psychological bulletin, 97(3), pp. 412.

HOCKING, J.E. and LEATHERS, D.G., 1980. Nonverbal indicators of deception: A new theoretical perspective. Communications Monographs, 47(2), pp. 119-131.

HOLLIEN, H.F., 1990. The acoustics of crime. Springer Science & Business Media.

ROCKWELL, P., BULLER, D.B. and BURGOON, J.K., 1997. The voice of deceit: Refining and expanding vocal cues to deception. Communication Research Reports, 14(4), pp. 451-459.

ZUCKERMAN, M., DEFRANK, R.S., HALL, J.A., LARRANCE, D.T. and ROSENTHAL, R., 1979. Facial and vocal cues of deception and honesty. Journal of experimental social psychology, 15(4), pp.

378-396.

Zuckerman, M., L.arrance, D. T., Spiegel, N. H., & Kiorman, R. (1981). Controlling nonverbal displays: Facial expressions and tone of voice. Journal of Experimental Social Psychology, 17, 506-524.

ZUCKERMAN, M., AMIDON, M.D., BISHOP, S.E. and POMERANTZ, S.D., 1982. Face and tone of voice in the communication of deception. Journal of personality and social psychology, 43(2), pp. 347.

Verbal Content :

7. Tense

BULLER, D.B. and BURGOON, J.K., 1996. Interpersonal deception theory. Communication theory, 6(3), pp. 203-242.

BURGOON, J.K. and QIN, T., 2006. The dynamic nature of deceptive verbal communication. Journal of Language and Social Psychology, 25(1), pp. 76-96

MATSUMOTO, D., HWANG, H.S., SKINNER, L. and FRANK, M., 2011. Evaluating truthfulness and detecting deception. FBI Law Enforcement Bulletin, 80, pp. 1-25.

PENNEBAKER, J.W., 2011. The secret life of pronouns. New Scientist, 211(2828), pp. 42-45.

ZUCKERMAN, M., DEPAULO, B.M. and ROSENTHAL, R., 1981. Verbal and nonverbal communication of deception. Advances in experimental social psychology, 14, pp. 1-59.

8. Distancing

BULLER, D.B. and BURGOON, J.K., 1996. Interpersonal deception theory. Communication theory, 6(3), pp. 203-242.

BURGOON, J.K. and QIN, T., 2006. The dynamic nature of deceptive verbal communication. Journal of Language and Social Psychology, 25(1), pp. 76-96

CARPENTER, R.H., 1981. Stylistic analysis for law enforcement purposes: A case study of a language variable as an index of a suspect's caution in phrasing answers. Communication Quarterly, 29(1), pp. 32-39.

COLWELL, K., HISCOCK, C.K. and MEMON, A., 2002. Interviewing techniques and the assessment of statement credibility. Applied Cognitive Psychology, 16(3), pp. 287-300.

COLWELL, K., HISCOCK-ANISMAN, C.K., MEMON, A., TAYLOR, L. and PREWETT, J., 2007. Assessment Criteria Indicative of Deception (ACID): An integrated system of investigative interviewing and detecting deception. Journal of Investigative Psychology and Offender Profiling, 4(3), pp. 167-180.

EKMAN, P., 2009. Telling Lies: Clues to Deceit in the Marketplace, Politics, and Marriage (Revised Edition). WW Norton & Company.

PEACE, K.A., SHUDRA, R.D., FORRESTER, D.L., KASPER, R., HARDER, J. and PORTER, S., 2014. Tall Tales Across Time: Narrative Analysis of True and False Allegations. Journal of Investigative Psychology and Offender Profiling, .

PENNEBAKER, J.W., 2011. The secret life of pronouns. New Scientist, 211(2828), pp. 42-45.

PORTER, S. and BRINKE, L., 2010. The truth about lies: What works in detecting high-stakes deception? Legal and Criminological Psychology, 15(1), pp. 57-75.

PORTER, S. and YUILLE, J.C., 1994. Credibility assessment of criminal suspects through statement analysis. Psychology, Crime and Law, 1(4), pp. 319-331.

9. Statement analysis (CBCA)

AKEHURST, L., KÖHNKEN, G. and HÖFER, E., 2001. Content credibility of accounts derived from live and video presentations. Legal and Criminological Psychology, 6(1), pp. 65-83.

BULLER, D.B. and BURGOON, J.K., 1996. Interpersonal deception theory. Communication theory, 6(3), pp. 203-242.

COLWELL, K., HISCOCK, C.K. and MEMON, A., 2002. Interviewing techniques and the assessment of statement credibility. Applied Cognitive Psychology, 16(3), pp. 287-300.

COLWELL, K., HISCOCK-ANISMAN, C.K., MEMON, A., TAYLOR, L. and PREWETT, J., 2007. Assessment Criteria Indicative of Deception (ACID): An integrated system of investigative interviewing and detecting deception. Journal of Investigative Psychology and Offender Profiling, 4(3), pp. 167-180.

KNIEPS, M., GRANHAG, P. and VRIJ, A., 2013. Repeated visits to the future: Asking about mental images to discriminate between true and false intentions. International Journal of Advances in Psychology, 2(2), pp. 93.

MCDOUGALL, A.J. and BULL, R., 2014. Detecting truth in suspect interviews: The effect of use of evidence (early and gradual) and time delay on Criteria-Based Content Analysis, Reality monitoring and inconsistency within suspect statements. Psychology, Crime & Law, (just-accepted), pp. 1-26.

PEACE, K.A., SHUDRA, R.D., FORRESTER, D.L., KASPER, R., HARDER, J. and PORTER, S., 2014. Tall Tales Across Time: Narrative Analysis of True and False Allegations. Journal of Investigative Psychology and Offender Profiling, .

PENNEBAKER, J.W., 2011. The secret life of pronouns. New Scientist, 211(2828), pp. 42-45.

PORTER, S. and BRINKE, L., 2010. The truth about lies: What works in detecting high-stakes deception? Legal and Criminological Psychology, 15(1), pp. 57-75.

PORTER, S. and YUILLE, J.C., 1994. Credibility assessment of criminal suspects through statement analysis. Psychology, Crime and Law, 1(4), pp. 319-331.

UNDEUTSCH, U., 1989. The development of statement reality analysis. Credibility assessment. Springer, pp. 101-119.

VRIJ, A., EDWARD, K., ROBERTS, K.P. and BULL, R., 2000. Detecting deceit via analysis of verbal and nonverbal behaviour. Journal of Nonverbal Behaviour, 24(4), pp. 239-263.

YUILLE, J.C. and CUTSHALL, J., 1989. Analysis of the statements of victims, witnesses and suspects. Credibility assessment. Springer, pp. 175-191.

10. Verbal slip

EKMAN, P., 2009. Telling Lies: Clues to Deceit in the Marketplace, Politics, and Marriage (Revised Edition). WW Norton & Company.

WOJCIECHOWSKI, J., STOLARSKI, M. and MATTHEWS, G., 2014. Emotional Intelligence and Mismatching Expressive and Verbal Messages: A Contribution to Detection of Deception. PloS one, 9(3), pp. e92570.

ZUCKERMAN, M., DEPAULO, B.M. and ROSENTHAL, R., 1981. Verbal and nonverbal communication of deception. Advances in experimental social psychology, 14, pp. 1-59.

Facial Expression:

11. FACS (Facial Action Coding System) Anomaly

BULLER, D.B. and BURGOON, J.K., 1996. Interpersonal deception theory. Communication theory, 6(3), pp. 203-242.

EKMAN, P. and FRIESEN, W.V., 1969. Nonverbal leakage and clues to deception, .

EKMAN, P. and FRIESEN, W.V., 1974. Detecting deception from

the body or face. *Journal of personality and social psychology,* 29(3), pp. 288.

EKMAN, P., FRIESEN, W.V., O'SULLIVAN, M. and SCHERER, K., 1980. Relative importance of face, body, and speech in judgments of personality and affect. *Journal of personality and social psychology,* 38(2), pp. 270.

EKMAN, P., 2003. Darwin, deception, and facial expression. *Annals of the New York Academy of Sciences,* 1000(1), pp. 205-221.

EKMAN, P., 2007. *Emotions revealed: Recognizing faces and feelings to improve communication and emotional life.* Macmillan.

EKMAN, P., 2009. *Telling Lies: Clues to Deceit in the Marketplace, Politics, and Marriage (Revised Edition).* WW Norton & Company.

ELFENBEIN, H.A. and AMBADY, N., 2002. On the universality and cultural specificity of emotion recognition: a meta-analysis. *Psychological bulletin,* 128(2), pp. 203.

FRANK, M.G. and EKMAN, P., 1993. Not all smiles are created equal: The differences between enjoyment and nonenjoyment smiles. *Humor: International Journal of Humor Research.*

FRANK, M.G. and EKMAN, P., 2004. Appearing truthful generalizes across different deception situations. *Journal of personality and social psychology,* 86(3), pp. 486.

MATSUMOTO, D., HWANG, H.S., SKINNER, L. and FRANK, M., 2011. Evaluating truthfulness and detecting deception. *FBI Law Enforcement Bulletin,* 80, pp. 1-25.

PORTER, S. and BRINKE, L., 2010. The truth about lies: What works in detecting high-stakes deception? *Legal and Criminological Psychology,* 15(1), pp. 57-75.

TEN BRINKE, L., MACDONALD, S., PORTER, S. and O'CONNOR, B., 2012. Crocodile tears: Facial, verbal and body language behaviours associated with genuine and fabricated remorse. *Law and human behaviour,* 36(1), pp. 51.

VRIJ, A., EDWARD, K., ROBERTS, K.P. and BULL, R., 2000. Detecting deceit via analysis of verbal and nonverbal behaviour. Journal of Nonverbal Behaviour, 24(4), pp. 239-263.

WOJCIECHOWSKI, J., STOLARSKI, M. and MATTHEWS, G., 2014. Emotional Intelligence and Mismatching Expressive and Verbal Messages: A Contribution to Detection of Deception. PloS one, 9(3), pp. e92570.

YAP, M.H., RAJOUB, B., UGAIL, H. and ZWIGGELAAR, R., 2011. Visual cues of facial behaviour in deception detection, Computer Applications and Industrial Electronics (ICCAIE), 2011 IEEE International Conference on 2011, IEEE, pp. 294-299.

ZUCKERMAN, M., DEFRANK, R.S., HALL, J.A., LARRANCE, D.T. and ROSENTHAL, R., 1979. Facial and vocal cues of deception and honesty. Journal of experimental social psychology, 15(4), pp. 378-396.

Zuckerman, M., L.arrance, D. T., Spiegel, N. H., & Kiorman, R. (1981). Controlling nonverbal displays: Facial expressions and tone of voice. Journal of Experimental Social Psychology, 17, 506-524.

ZUCKERMAN, M., AMIDON, M.D., BISHOP, S.E. and POMERANTZ, S.D., 1982. Face and tone of voice in the communication of deception. Journal of personality and social psychology, 43(2), pp. 347.

12. Duration of the expression

EKMAN, P. and FRIESEN, W.V., 1969. Nonverbal leakage and clues to deception, .

EKMAN, P. and FRIESEN, W.V., 1974. Detecting deception from the body or face. Journal of personality and social psychology, 29(3), pp. 288.

EKMAN, P., 2003. Darwin, deception, and facial expression.

Annals of the New York Academy of Sciences, 1000(1), pp. 205-221.

EKMAN, P., 2009. Telling Lies: Clues to Deceit in the Marketplace, Politics, and Marriage (Revised Edition). WW Norton & Company.

FRANK, M.G. and EKMAN, P., 1993. Not all smiles are created equal: The differences between enjoyment and nonenjoyment smiles. Humor: International Journal of Humor Research.

MATSUMOTO, D., HWANG, H.S., SKINNER, L. and FRANK, M., 2011. Evaluating truthfulness and detecting deception. FBI Law Enforcement Bulletin, 80, pp. 1-25.

TEN BRINKE, L., MACDONALD, S., PORTER, S. and O'CONNOR, B., 2012. Crocodile tears: Facial, verbal and body language behaviours associated with genuine and fabricated remorse. Law and human behaviour, 36(1), pp. 51.

13. Symmetry across the face

EKMAN, P., 2003. Darwin, deception, and facial expression. Annals of the New York Academy of Sciences, 1000(1), pp. 205-221.

FRANK, M.G. and EKMAN, P., 1993. Not all smiles are created equal: The differences between enjoyment and nonenjoyment smiles. Humor: International Journal of Humor Research.

14. Synchrony between muscles

EKMAN, P., 2003. Darwin, deception, and facial expression. Annals of the New York Academy of Sciences, 1000(1), pp. 205-221.

FRANK, M.G. and EKMAN, P., 1993. Not all smiles are created equal: The differences between enjoyment and nonenjoyment smiles. Humor: International Journal of Humor Research.

TEN BRINKE, L., MACDONALD, S., PORTER, S. and O'CONNOR, B., 2012. Crocodile tears: Facial, verbal and body language behaviours associated with genuine and fabricated remorse. Law and human behaviour, 36(1), pp. 51.

15. Profile of the onset-duration-offset of the expression

EKMAN, P., 2003. Darwin, deception, and facial expression. Annals of the New York Academy of Sciences, 1000(1), pp. 205-221.
FRANK, M.G. and EKMAN, P., 1993. Not all smiles are created equal: The differences between enjoyment and nonenjoyment smiles. Humor: International Journal of Humor Research.
TEN BRINKE, L., MACDONALD, S., PORTER, S. and O'CONNOR, B., 2012. Crocodile tears: Facial, verbal and body language behaviours associated with genuine and fabricated remorse. Law and human behaviour, 36(1), pp. 51.

Body Language:

16. Gestural slip

EKMAN, P. and FRIESEN, W.V., 1974. Detecting deception from the body or face. Journal of personality and social psychology, 29(3), pp. 288.
EKMAN, P., FRIESEN, W.V., O'SULLIVAN, M. and SCHERER, K., 1980. Relative importance of face, body, and speech in judgments of personality and affect. Journal of personality and social psychology, 38(2), pp. 270. E
KMAN, P., 2003. Darwin, deception, and facial expression. Annals of the New York Academy of Sciences, 1000(1), pp. 205-221.

EKMAN, P., 2009. *Telling Lies: Clues to Deceit in the Marketplace, Politics, and Marriage (Revised Edition)*. WW Norton & Company.

KENDON, A., 1983. Gesture and speech: How they interact. *Nonverbal interaction*, 11, pp. 13-45.

PORTER, S. and BRINKE, L., 2010. The truth about lies: What works in detecting high-stakes deception? *Legal and Criminological Psychology*, 15(1), pp. 57-75.

17. Illustrators

BULLER, D.B. and BURGOON, J.K., 1996. Interpersonal deception theory. *Communication theory*, 6(3), pp. 203-242.

BURGOON, J.K. and BULLER, D.B., 1994. Interpersonal deception: III. Effects of deceit on perceived communication and nonverbal behaviour dynamics. *Journal of Nonverbal Behaviour*, 18(2), pp. 155-184.

DEPAULO, B.M., LINDSAY, J.J., MALONE, B.E., MUHLENBRUCK, L., CHARLTON, K. and COOPER, H., 2003. Cues to deception. *Psychological bulletin*, 129(1), pp. 74.

EKMAN, P. and FRIESEN, W.V., 1969. Nonverbal leakage and clues to deception, .

EKMAN, P. and FRIESEN, W.V., 1974. Detecting deception from the body or face. *Journal of personality and social psychology*, 29(3), pp. 288.

EKMAN, P., FRIESEN, W.V., O'SULLIVAN, M. and SCHERER, K., 1980. Relative importance of face, body, and speech in judgments of personality and affect. *Journal of personality and social psychology*, 38(2), pp. 270.

EKMAN, P., 2003. Darwin, deception, and facial expression. *Annals of the New York Academy of Sciences*, 1000(1), pp. 205-221.

EKMAN, P., 2009. *Telling Lies: Clues to Deceit in the Marketplace,*

Politics, and Marriage (Revised Edition). WW Norton & Company.
EKMAN, P., FRIESEN, W.V. and SCHERER, K.R., 1976. Body
movement and voice pitch in deceptive interaction. Semiotica,
16(1), pp. 23-28.
KENDON, A., 1983. Gesture and speech: How they interact.
Nonverbal interaction, 11, pp. 13-45.
PORTER, S. and BRINKE, L., 2010. The truth about lies: What works
in detecting high-stakes deception? Legal and Criminological
Psychology, 15(1), pp. 57-75.
VRIJ, A., EDWARD, K., ROBERTS, K.P. and BULL, R., 2000. Detecting
deceit via analysis of verbal and nonverbal behaviour. Journal of
Nonverbal Behaviour, 24(4), pp. 239-263.
TEN BRINKE, L., MACDONALD, S., PORTER, S. and O'CONNOR, B.,
2012. Crocodile tears: Facial, verbal and body language
behaviours associated with genuine and fabricated remorse. Law
and human behaviour, 36(1), pp. 51.

18. Manipulators

BULLER, D.B. and BURGOON, J.K., 1996. Interpersonal deception
theory. Communication theory, 6(3), pp. 203-242.
BURGOON, J.K. and BULLER, D.B., 1994. Interpersonal deception:
III. Effects of deceit on perceived communication and nonverbal
behaviour dynamics. Journal of Nonverbal Behaviour, 18(2), pp.
155-184.
DEPAULO, B.M., LINDSAY, J.J., MALONE, B.E., MUHLENBRUCK, L.,
CHARLTON, K. and COOPER, H., 2003. Cues to deception.
Psychological bulletin, 129(1), pp. 74.
EKMAN, P. and FRIESEN, W.V., 1969. Nonverbal leakage and clues
to deception, .
EKMAN, P. and FRIESEN, W.V., 1974. Detecting deception from
the body or face. Journal of personality and social psychology,

29(3), pp. 288.

EKMAN, P., FRIESEN, W.V. and SCHERER, K.R., 1976. Body movement and voice pitch in deceptive interaction. Semiotica, 16(1), pp. 23-28.

EKMAN, P., FRIESEN, W.V., O'SULLIVAN, M. and SCHERER, K., 1980. Relative importance of face, body, and speech in judgments of personality and affect. Journal of personality and social psychology, 38(2), pp. 270.

EKMAN, P., 2009. Telling Lies: Clues to Deceit in the Marketplace, Politics, and Marriage (Revised Edition). WW Norton & Company.

KENDON, A., 1983. Gesture and speech: How they interact. Nonverbal interaction, 11, pp. 13-45.

VRIJ, A., EDWARD, K., ROBERTS, K.P. and BULL, R., 2000. Detecting deceit via analysis of verbal and nonverbal behaviour. Journal of Nonverbal Behaviour, 24(4), pp. 239-263.

TEN BRINKE, L., MACDONALD, S., PORTER, S. and O'CONNOR, B., 2012. Crocodile tears: Facial, verbal and body language behaviours associated with genuine and fabricated remorse. Law and human behaviour, 36(1), pp. 51.

VRIJ, A., EDWARD, K., ROBERTS, K.P. and BULL, R., 2000. Detecting deceit via analysis of verbal and nonverbal behaviour. Journal of Nonverbal Behaviour, 24(4), pp. 239-263.

19. Tension

EKMAN, P. and FRIESEN, W.V., 1969. Nonverbal leakage and clues to deception, .

EKMAN, P. and FRIESEN, W.V., 1974. Detecting deception from the body or face. Journal of personality and social psychology, 29(3), pp. 288.

EKMAN, P., 2009. Telling Lies: Clues to Deceit in the Marketplace, Politics, and Marriage (Revised Edition). WW Norton & Company.

KENDON, A., 1983. Gesture and speech: How they interact. Nonverbal interaction, 11, pp. 13-45.

TEN BRINKE, L., MACDONALD, S., PORTER, S. and O'CONNOR, B., 2012. Crocodile tears: Facial, verbal and body language behaviours associated with genuine and fabricated remorse. Law and human behaviour, 36(1), pp. 51.

VRIJ, A., EDWARD, K., ROBERTS, K.P. and BULL, R., 2000. Detecting deceit via analysis of verbal and nonverbal behaviour. Journal of Nonverbal Behaviour, 24(4), pp. 239-263.

20. Eyes

BULLER, D.B. and BURGOON, J.K., 1996. Interpersonal deception theory. Communication theory, 6(3), pp. 203-242.

BURGOON, J.K. and BULLER, D.B., 1994. Interpersonal deception: III. Effects of deceit on perceived communication and nonverbal behaviour dynamics. Journal of Nonverbal Behaviour, 18(2), pp. 155-184.

DRISKELL, J.E., SALAS, E. and DRISKELL, T., 2012. Social indicators of deception. Human factors, 54(4), pp. 577-588.

LEAL, S. and VRIJ, A., 2008. Blinking during and after lying. Journal of Nonverbal Behaviour, 32(4), pp. 187-194.

MANN, S., VRIJ, A. and BULL, R., 2002. Suspects, lies, and videotape: An analysis of authentic high-stake liars. Law and human behaviour, 26(3), pp. 365-376.

PORTER, S. and BRINKE, L., 2010. The truth about lies: What works in detecting high-stakes deception? Legal and Criminological Psychology, 15(1), pp. 57-75.

VRIJ, A., EDWARD, K., ROBERTS, K.P. and BULL, R., 2000. Detecting deceit via analysis of verbal and nonverbal behaviour. Journal of Nonverbal Behaviour, 24(4), pp. 239-263.

ZUCKERMAN, M., DEPAULO, B.M. and ROSENTHAL, R., 1981.

Verbal and nonverbal communication of deception. Advances in experimental social psychology, 14, pp. 1-59.

Psychophysiology:

21. Heart rate

CRITCHLEY, H.D., ECCLES, J. and GARFINKEL, S.N., 2013. Interaction between cognition, emotion, and the autonomic nervous system. Handb Clin Neurol, 117, pp. 59-77.

EKMAN, P., LEVENSON, R.W. and FRIESEN, W.V., 1983. Autonomic nervous system activity distinguishes among emotions. Science (New York, N.Y.), 221(4616), pp. 1208-1210.

GROSS, J.J. and LEVENSON, R.W., 1997. Hiding feelings: the acute effects of inhibiting negative and positive emotion. Journal of abnormal psychology, 106(1), pp. 95.

GUSTAFSON, L.A. and ORNE, M.T., 1963. Effects of heightened motivation on the detection of deception. Journal of Applied Psychology, 47(6), pp. 408.

KREIBIG, S.D., 2010. Autonomic nervous system activity in emotion: A review. Biological psychology, 84(3), pp. 394-421.

LEVENSON, R.W., 2014. The Autonomic Nervous System and Emotion. Emotion Review, 6(2), pp. 100-112.

PALMATIER, J.J. and ROVNER, L., 2014. Credibility assessment: Preliminary Process Theory, the polygraph process, and construct validity. International Journal of Psychophysiology (2014).

PODLESNY, J.A. and RASKIN, D.C., 1977. Physiological measures and the detection of deception. Psychological bulletin, 84(4), pp. 782.

SHIOTA, M.N., NEUFELD, S.L., YEUNG, W.H., MOSER, S.E. and PEREA, E.F., 2011. Feeling good: autonomic nervous system responding in five positive emotions. Emotion, 11(6), pp. 1368.

THACKRAY, R.I. and ORNE, M.T., 1968. A COMPARISON OF
PHYSIOLOGICAL INDICES IN DETECTION OE DECEPTION.
Psychophysiology, 4(3), pp. 329-339.

22. Galvonomic

CRITCHLEY, H.D., ECCLES, J. and GARFINKEL, S.N., 2013.
Interaction between cognition, emotion, and the autonomic
nervous system. Handb Clin Neurol, 117, pp. 59-77.
EKMAN, P., LEVENSON, R.W. and FRIESEN, W.V., 1983. Autonomic
nervous system activity distinguishes among emotions. Science
(New York, N.Y.), 221(4616), pp. 1208-1210.
GROSS, J.J. and LEVENSON, R.W., 1997. Hiding feelings: the acute
effects of inhibiting negative and positive emotion. Journal of
abnormal psychology, 106(1), pp. 95.
GUSTAFSON, L.A. and ORNE, M.T., 1963. Effects of heightened
motivation on the detection of deception. Journal of Applied
Psychology, 47(6), pp. 408.
KREIBIG, S.D., 2010. Autonomic nervous system activity in
emotion: A review. Biological psychology, 84(3), pp. 394-421.
LEVENSON, R.W., 2014. The Autonomic Nervous System and
Emotion. Emotion Review, 6(2), pp. 100-112.
PALMATIER, J.J. and ROVNER, L., 2014. Credibility assessment:
Preliminary Process Theory, the polygraph process, and construct
validity. International Journal of Psychophysiology (2014).
PODLESNY, J.A. and RASKIN, D.C., 1977. Physiological measures
and the detection of deception. Psychological bulletin, 84(4), pp.
782.
SHI, Y., RUIZ, N., TAIB, R., CHOI, E. and CHEN, F., 2007. Galvanic
skin response (GSR) as an index of cognitive load, CHI'07 extended
abstracts on Human factors in computing systems 2007, ACM, pp.
2651-2656.

SHIOTA, M.N., NEUFELD, S.L., YEUNG, W.H., MOSER, S.E. and PEREA, E.F., 2011. Feeling good: autonomic nervous system responding in five positive emotions. Emotion, 11(6), pp. 1368.

THACKRAY, R.I. and ORNE, M.T., 1968. A COMPARISON OF PHYSIOLOGICAL INDICES IN DETECTION OE DECEPTION. Psychophysiology, 4(3), pp. 329-339.

23. Temperature

Pavlidis I., Eberhardt N. L., Levine J. A. (2002). Seeing through the face of deception. Nature 415:35 10.1038/415035a

Pavlidis I., Levine J. (2002). Thermal image analysis for polygraph testing. IEEE Eng. Med. Biol. Mag. 21, 56–64

Pollina D. A., Dollins A. B., Senter S. M., Brown T. E., Pavlidis I., Levine J. A., et al. (2006). Facial skin surface temperature changes during a "Concealed Information" Test. Ann. Biomed. Eng. 7, 1182–1189 10.1007/s10439-006-9143-3

PRITCHARD, D.A., 1990. An infrared imaging area sensor for tactical and physical security applications. No. SAND-90-0494. Sandia National Labs., Albuquerque, NM (USA), 1990.

Tsiamyrtzis P., Dowdall J., Shastri D., Pavlidis I. T., Frank M. G., Ekman P. (2007). Imaging facial physiology for the detection of deceit. Int. J. Comput. Vis. 71, 197–214

24. Blood pressure

CRITCHLEY, H.D., ECCLES, J. and GARFINKEL, S.N., 2013. Interaction between cognition, emotion, and the autonomic nervous system. Handb Clin Neurol, 117, pp. 59-77.

EKMAN, P., LEVENSON, R.W. and FRIESEN, W.V., 1983. Autonomic nervous system activity distinguishes among emotions. Science

(New York, N.Y.), 221(4616), pp. 1208-1210.

GROSS, J.J. and LEVENSON, R.W., 1997. Hiding feelings: the acute effects of inhibiting negative and positive emotion. Journal of abnormal psychology, 106(1), pp. 95.

GUSTAFSON, L.A. and ORNE, M.T., 1963. Effects of heightened motivation on the detection of deception. Journal of Applied Psychology, 47(6), pp. 408.

KREIBIG, S.D., 2010. Autonomic nervous system activity in emotion: A review. Biological psychology, 84(3), pp. 394-421.

LEVENSON, R.W., 2014. The Autonomic Nervous System and Emotion. Emotion Review, 6(2), pp. 100-112.

PALMATIER, J.J. and ROVNER, L., 2014. Credibility assessment: Preliminary Process Theory, the polygraph process, and construct validity. International Journal of Psychophysiology (2014).

PODLESNY, J.A. and RASKIN, D.C., 1977. Physiological measures and the detection of deception. Psychological bulletin, 84(4), pp. 782.

SHI, Y., RUIZ, N., TAIB, R., CHOI, E. and CHEN, F., 2007. Galvanic skin response (GSR) as an index of cognitive load, CHI'07 extended abstracts on Human factors in computing systems 2007, ACM, pp. 2651-2656.

SHIOTA, M.N., NEUFELD, S.L., YEUNG, W.H., MOSER, S.E. and PEREA, E.F., 2011. Feeling good: autonomic nervous system responding in five positive emotions. Emotion, 11(6), pp. 1368.

THACKRAY, R.I. and ORNE, M.T., 1968. A COMPARISON OF PHYSIOLOGICAL INDICES IN DETECTION OE DECEPTION. Psychophysiology, 4(3), pp. 329-339.

25. Breathing

CRITCHLEY, H.D., ECCLES, J. and GARFINKEL, S.N., 2013. Interaction between cognition, emotion, and the autonomic nervous system. *Handb Clin Neurol*, 117, pp. 59-77.

EKMAN, P., LEVENSON, R.W. and FRIESEN, W.V., 1983. Autonomic nervous system activity distinguishes among emotions. *Science (New York, N.Y.)*, 221(4616), pp. 1208-1210.

GROSS, J.J. and LEVENSON, R.W., 1997. Hiding feelings: the acute effects of inhibiting negative and positive emotion. *Journal of abnormal psychology*, 106(1), pp. 95.

GUSTAFSON, L.A. and ORNE, M.T., 1963. Effects of heightened motivation on the detection of deception. *Journal of Applied Psychology*, 47(6), pp. 408.

KREIBIG, S.D., 2010. Autonomic nervous system activity in emotion: A review. *Biological psychology*, 84(3), pp. 394-421.

LEVENSON, R.W., 2014. The Autonomic Nervous System and Emotion. *Emotion Review*, 6(2), pp. 100-112.

PALMATIER, J.J. and ROVNER, L., 2014. Credibility assessment: Preliminary Process Theory, the polygraph process, and construct validity. *International Journal of Psychophysiology* (2014).

PODLESNY, J.A. and RASKIN, D.C., 1977. Physiological measures and the detection of deception. *Psychological bulletin*, 84(4), pp. 782.

SHI, Y., RUIZ, N., TAIB, R., CHOI, E. and CHEN, F., 2007. Galvanic skin response (GSR) as an index of cognitive load, CHI'07 extended abstracts on Human factors in computing systems 2007, ACM, pp. 2651-2656.

SHIOTA, M.N., NEUFELD, S.L., YEUNG, W.H., MOSER, S.E. and PEREA, E.F., 2011. Feeling good: autonomic nervous system responding in five positive emotions. *Emotion*, 11(6), pp. 1368.

THACKRAY, R.I. and ORNE, M.T., 1968. A COMPARISON OF PHYSIOLOGICAL INDICES IN DETECTION OE DECEPTION. *Psychophysiology*, 4(3), pp. 329-339.

26. Digestion

CRITCHLEY, H.D., ECCLES, J. and GARFINKEL, S.N., 2013. Interaction between cognition, emotion, and the autonomic nervous system. Handb Clin Neurol, 117, pp. 59-77.

EKMAN, P., LEVENSON, R.W. and FRIESEN, W.V., 1983. Autonomic nervous system activity distinguishes among emotions. Science (New York, N.Y.), 221(4616), pp. 1208-1210.

GROSS, J.J. and LEVENSON, R.W., 1997. Hiding feelings: the acute effects of inhibiting negative and positive emotion. Journal of abnormal psychology, 106(1), pp. 95.

GUSTAFSON, L.A. and ORNE, M.T., 1963. Effects of heightened motivation on the detection of deception. Journal of Applied Psychology, 47(6), pp. 408.

KREIBIG, S.D., 2010. Autonomic nervous system activity in emotion: A review. Biological psychology, 84(3), pp. 394-421.

LEVENSON, R.W., 2014. The Autonomic Nervous System and Emotion. Emotion Review, 6(2), pp. 100-112.

PASRICHA, .T, SALLAM, H., CHEN, J., PASRICHA, P.J., 2008. The moment of truth: Stress, Lying and the GI Tract. Expert Rev. Gastroenterol. Hepatol. 2(3), 291-293.

PODLESNY, J.A. and RASKIN, D.C., 1977. Physiological measures and the detection of deception. Psychological bulletin, 84(4), pp. 782.

SHIOTA, M.N., NEUFELD, S.L., YEUNG, W.H., MOSER, S.E. and PEREA, E.F., 2011. Feeling good: autonomic nervous system responding in five positive emotions. Emotion, 11(6), pp. 1368.

THACKRAY, R.I. and ORNE, M.T., 1968. A comparison of physiological indices in detection of deception. Psychophysiology, 4(3), pp. 329-339.

27. Pupils.

DIONISIO, D. P. GRANHOLM, E. HILLIX, W. A. AND PERRINE, W.F.

"Differentiation of Deception Using Pupillary Responses as an Index of Cognitive Processing." Psychophysiology, 2001, 38(2), pp. 205-11.

HEILVEIL, I. "Deception and Pupil Size." Journal of Clinical Psychology, 1976, 32(3), pp. 675-76.

JANISSE, M.P. AND BRADLEY, M. T. "Deception, Information and the Pupillary Response." Perceptual and Motor Skills, 1980, 50(3), pp. 748-50.

LUBOW, R. E. AND FEIN, OFER. "Pupillary Size in Response to a Visual Guilty Knowledge Test: 34 New Technique for the Detection of Deception." Journal of Experimental Psychology-Applied, 1996, 2(2), pp. 164-77.

WEBB, A.K. HACKER, D.J. OSHER, D. COOK, A.E. WOLTZ, D.J. KRISTJANSSON, S. KIRCHER, J.C. "Eye movements and pupil size reveal deception in computer administered questionnaires". In: Schmorrow, D.D. Estabrooke, I.V. Grootjen, M. editors. Foundations of Augmented Cognition. Neuroergonomics and Operational Neuroscience. Springer-Verlag; Berlin/Heidelberg: 2009. pp. 553–562.

Appendix III – Glossary of Terms

Term	Explanation (in context of Behaviour Analysis – often not pure dictionary definitions)
Affect	A scientific term for feeling or emotion.
Affect Programme	An inherited central mechanism that (Silvan Tomkins argues) directs emotional impulses and behaviour following a trigger of an emotion.
Amnesia	A partial or complete loss of memory, usually caused by psychological or physical trauma.
Amygdala	A region of the brain that plays a vital role in planning, processing and executing emotions.
Anger	A strong feeling or emotion caused by an interference with our goals, e.g. a physical threat, insult or breach of our morals or values.
Attribution Theory	Attributing cause to events around us. In errors, we often attribute internal factors for others; external factors/context for self
Autonomic Nervous System	Part of the body which regulates heart rate, breathing, sweating, etc to help prepare

the body for action.

Anthropology The study of humankind and our divergence from other animals.

Asperger's Syndrome A disorder characterised by significant difficulties with social interaction and non-verbal communication.

Attentiveness The ability to pay appropriate attention to something in the present moment.

Autism A disorder characterised by self-absorption and a diminished ability to respond and interact with others.

Automatic Appraisal The theory that emotions derive from our automatic evaluations of specific triggers or events that can lead onto subconscious or conscious reactions and responses to those events.

Baseline A person, group or contextual 'norm' that acts as a basis for comparison.

Base-rate A measurement of the probability with which an event will/may occur.

Behavioural Detection Officer An individual who observes people (e.g. in an airport) in order to detect any unusual or suspicious behaviour.

Behavioural Science The study of the interactions and activities of humans and animals.

Bias

A prejudiced tendency to take 'short cuts' or lean towards a specific conclusion or position.

Biometrics

The application of statistical analysis to biological data during the study of organisms.

Blanch

When an individual's skin colour may be affected by blood circulation moving away from the skin surface.

Blend

Two or more emotions merging together.

Blood Pressure

The pressure applied by blood against the artery walls that is measured as the pressure when the heart is contracting over the pressure when relaxing. It can be affected by age, health and stressful situations.

Blood Volume

The volume of blood in the circulatory system of an individual. Typically, an adult should have a blood volume of approximately 4.7-5litres, with females usually having less volume than their male counterparts.

Blush or Flush

When an individual's skin colour may be affected by blood circulation moving towards the skin surface.

Body Language

A form of nonverbal communication which can be portrayed through conscious or unconscious movements and gestures from the body.

Botox
A neurotoxin which is injected into the face in small quantities in order to treat muscle spasms and reduce wrinkles by relaxing the facial muscles.

Brokaw Hazard
An incident where a lie-catcher does not take into account the fact that there may be individual differences in emotional expressions (Ekman description of interviewer Tom Brokaw's bias).

Carotid Artery
Either of two major arteries located on either side of the neck which carry the blood to the head.

Cluster
Three or more PIns across two or more channels within 7 seconds of a stimulus – within the SCAnR model.

Criteria Based Content Analysis
A widely used technique involving various criteria for credibility which can help to distinguish between true and fabricated accounts.

Cognitive Interviewing
A type of technique used when questioning others in order to try and enhance the retrieval rate of information that can be remembered.

Cognitive Science
A term given to the various disciplines that study the human mind which encompass cognitive psychology, computer sciences,

neuropsychology etc.

Cold Reading A term given to the technique where one individual deduces information from another individual often to imply that the reader knows much more about the person than the reader actually does.

Communication The transference of a particular thing from one place to another. This could be a message, meaning or signal.

Communication Channels The various ways in which it is possible to communicate with someone.

Compassion A reaction to other people's emotions which causes us to sympathise and be concerned for others and their suffering.

Cognitive Load the total amount of mental effort being used in the working memory.

Concealed Information When an individual withholds information from others.

Convincing Statement A statement made in an attempt to convince others of our statement - often used when conveying the 'facts' don't help a liar.

Congruent When an individual has a healthy balance of their real self, perceived self and ideal self they are said to be congruent which leads on to self-actualization.

Consistent   When an individual acts or behaves (within a given context) in the same way over time and/or across communication channels during communication/behaviour episodes.

Contamination   The result of allowing previous or subsequent information to impact on the collection and analysis of data when in a current setting.

Contempt   A feeling of disapproval towards others from a feeling/position of moral superiority.

Context   The micro and macro circumstances around the event or conversational exchange.

Conversation Management   Basic principles and techniques of guiding a conversation with a purpose.

Corroborate   To give support to a claim, statement, theory or finding.

Covariation Model   Explaining behaviours based on similarities across a range of situations.

Credibility   The quality a person or thing may possess which makes them believable and/or worthy of trust.

Cultural   Relating to the social ideas, norms and behaviour of a society.

Disgust   A feeling of repulsion caused by something or someone unpleasant.

Disorder A popular term in psychiatry and clinical psychology meaning state of confusion or lack or order.

Display Rules Socially learned rules concerning how to manage expressions - for instance, which emotions can be shown to which people and when. These rules may differ from culture to culture and could mean that we sometimes mask our true emotions.

Electro-encephalography Or EEG. A way of gathering data which depicts the changes in electrical potential within the brain.

Emotional Intelligence Academy An organisation established to make high quality, science-based emotion/deception training accessible to those who need to know what others are thinking and feeling – and to help those working in high-stake contexts to judge when they are faced with lies or truth.

Emblems A term to describe certain signals humans make consciously or subconsciously with parts of the body that have meaning without words.

Emotion A brief subjective experience which happens to us, brought on by a trigger (real, imagined or relived) that can lead to physiological changes that have evolved to help us to deal with a situation that matters to our welfare.

Emotional   A term relating to the emotions meaning characterized by intense feeling.

Emotional Alert Database   A 'database' within the unconscious mind which stores events that have been relevant to our survival – both evolved and through personal experience - and the emotions associated triggers that resemble those events.

Emotional Intelligence   A term defined as the ability to recognise, assess and control one's own emotions and recognise, assess others' emotions and make conscious choices based on this information (often directed towards constructive cooperation).

Emotional Styles   An individual's natural pattern or usual emotional reaction to certain situations.

Empathy   When an individual can identify with, comprehend and feel the emotions held by another person or thing.

Empirical   Based upon observation or experiment as opposed to theory, allowing the findings to then be analysed quantitatively or qualitatively.

Emotional Awareness   The awareness of our own emotions and the emotions of other people.

Episodic   Containing or consisting of a series of separate parts or events. 'Episodic' memory is the narrative or story of a remembered event.

Evolution   The progressive development of something
                        from a simple form to a more complex
                        form.

Eye Accessing Cues The movements of the eyes in specific
                        directions that suggest that an individual is
                        thinking or accessing information from the
                        mind.

Face Anatomy   The physical structure of the face.

Facial Expression   The resulting change of facial features
                        following the movement of one or more of
                        the 43 muscles within the face that may
                        reflect emotions or cognitive processes.

Facial Action Coding Or FACS. Taxonomy of human facial
System   movements and their appearance on the
                        face - used in order to categorise the
                        physical expression following the
                        movement of the head, shoulders, eyes and
                        one or more of the muscles within the face.

False Negative   When a person or machine misjudges a lie
                        as true.

False Positive   When a person or machine misjudges a
                        truth as a lie.

Fear   An emotion that occurs as a result of the
                        threat of harm.

Functional Magnetic Or fMRI. A technique for measuring brain

Resonance Imaging   activity as a result of blood flow.

Forensic   The use of scientific methods, usually in order to investigate a crime. Literally, pertaining to a judicial or courtroom context.

Framing   An example of cognitive bias where individuals may react differently to specific choices due to a process of defining the context or issues that surround a problem or event in a way that serves to influence how the context or issues are seen and evaluated.

Galvanic Skin Response   Defined as the change in the resistance to electrical current flow of the skin, induced by stress and strong emotions such as fear.

Gesture   See Emblem.

Ground Truth   Whether or not an individual committed the act they are accused of or not. This is usually linked to the concept of lie detection.

Guilty Knowledge Test   A test that compares specific responses given by an individual to a variety of multiple choice questions about a crime with one of the choices containing information that only the investigators and the criminal would know.

Happy   An emotion described as the feeling of

pleasure and contentment.

Heart Rate The speed at which a person's heart is
beating, which is often measured to assess
a person's health or how their heartbeat
can change when asked specific questions.

Hedge A term defined as a verbal device which
functions as freeing the individual talking
from full responsibility of what they are
saying.

Heuristic A mental shortcut or bias that can allow
people to solve problems and make
judgments quickly and efficiently.

Hippocampus A sea-horse shaped structure which forms
part of the limbic system within the brain
and is involved with processing emotions
and memory.

H_0Tspot A name given by Paul Ekman to an
inconsistency across communication
channels and/or between behavioural signs
and what someone is attempting to
communicate - they are not necessarily
signs of deceit. A behavioural spot to
formulate and test hypotheses.

Hypnosis A term defined as a trance-like state similar
to sleep usually brought on by a therapist
that can raise the level of suggestibility in a
patient. It can be used in order to recover
repressed memories and modify unwanted

behaviour.

Idiosyncratic   A term defined as when an individual has a peculiar way of thought or type of behaviour.

Illustrators   A term used to describe the movements an individual may make which reinforce or illustrate speech – use to help explain what the individual is saying (usually movements of the hands).

Implicit   When something is alluded to, or inferred in communication but not directly expressed or stated. In memory types, 'implicit' memories are performance related and do not require conscious recall e.g. tying shoe-laces, riding a bike.

Impulse   The name given to an electrochemical transmission of a signal along a particular nerve resulting in a response at a muscle or another nerve. In emotional terms, this is the initial automatic, unbidden response within the brain and body on the triggering of an emotional response.

Intelligence   A term used to describe the ability to store and apply knowledgeable information and skills.

Intent   A term used to describe something deliberate: usually an aim or a purpose in advance of an action.

Interrogation   When an individual is asked a number of questions in an oppressive manner in order to obtain information - sometimes with the use of violence and threats.

Interview   A directed conversation for either information-gathering or therapeutic purposes.

Kinaesthetic   A term which describes the sensations felt in the muscles, joints and tendons which make up part of the sensory system.

Laser Vibrometer   A scientific instrument which is used to determine the vibration measurements of a surface.

Latency   Defined as a delay or a lapse in time.

Latency Response Rate   The length of time between a stimulus and the reaction response.

Layered Voice Analysis   A technology which aims to establish an individual's mental state and emotional makeup by looking at the emotional content of their speech when they are asked a series of questions. It can show stress levels, cognitive processes and emotional reactions.

Licensed Delivery Centre   A faculty which is licensed to train people in PEI courses.

Leading Question   A question which is constructed in such a way that it may suggest the answer which the person desires.

Leakage   A term given to signals which are given off one or more communication channels which may not be intended by the sender.

Lie   A deliberate attempt to mislead without giving prior notification.

Linguistics   The scientific study of language which focuses on the structure and content of what is said/written.

Machiavellian   A person who schemes, deceives or/and is cunning.

Malfaisant   A person intent on evil or harm

Manipulators   Defined as any movement where one part of the body picks, holds, rubs, scratches, etc, another part of the body.

Meditation   A practice where an individual trains the mind or induces a mode of consciousness, either to realize some benefit or for the mind to simply acknowledge its content without becoming identified with that content, or as an end in itself.

Memory   The ability of the mind to collect and recall past events, sensations, knowledge and thoughts.

METT   An interactive online tool that helps to improve an individual's ability to notice micro expressions.

Mind   The part of a person that enables consciousness, perception, judgement, thinking and memory.

Mindfulness   Paying attention in a particular way: on purpose, in the present moment and non-judgementally. (Jon Kabat-Zinn).

Mind Virus   A hypothetical statement or question used to establish truth. "is it possible..."; "Is there any reason that...".

Mirror Neurons Mirror neurons in the premotor cortex are responsive when we perform a specific action as well as when we see another individual performing that same action.

Mood   Defined as a temporary state of mind or feeling.

Motivation   Defined as the reason why an individual chooses to act or behave in a particular way.

Motives   Defined as states of arousal which cause an individual to behave in a certain way or do a certain thing.

Narcissist   A person who pursues gratification from vanity or egotistic admiration of one's own attributes.

Neurons Derived from the word *neuro* meaning relating to a nerve a nerve cell makes up the basic structural and functional unit within the nervous system.

Neuro-Linguistic Programming An approach which focuses on personal development, psychotherapy and communication. The pioneers of this approach stated that there is a connection between neurological processes, language and behaviour learnt through experience and these can be changed to achieve goals.

Non Verbal Communication Defined as the use of communication which is neither written or spoken in order to put across a meaning.

Othello Error When an individual jumps to conclusions about why a person is feeling a particular emotion.

PEACE A UK police force model used in interview processes in order to gather information and minimise miscarriages of justice and false confessions. P - Planning and preparation; E - Engage and explain; A - Account, clarification and Challenge; C - Closure; E - Evaluation.

PEEVR A model developed by EIA, on from the PEER model pioneered by Paul Ekman International, which helps an individual prepare for any emotionally charged encounters they might have. This model focuses on planning and preparation, engagement, exploration, verification, and resolution.

Paul Ekman International	A company set up in 2009 in order for anyone to be able to learn from the science and work of Dr Paul Ekman.
Personality	Defined as various qualities that combine together in order to label an individual's character.
Points of Interest	Or PIns. A name given to an inconsistency between communication channels and what someone is attempting to communicate, and/or their baseline and/or the context - they are not necessarily signs of deceit.
Polygraph	A machine which is designed to record changes in an individual's physiological characteristics. Measures stress/anxiety – not reliable for general lie detection as it only relates to one channel (Psychophysiology).
Posture	Defined as the position of an individual's body when they are either standing or seated.
Pre-Frontal Cortex	Described as the grey matter of the anterior part of the frontal lobe of the brain. Its role is to regulate complex

emotional, cognitive and behavioural functioning.

Probes A stimulus, usually as a question, used in interviews to test hypotheses around what people are thinking and feeling.

Projection In psychoanalysis terms it is defined as when an individual ascribes their own traits or emotions onto another person.

Psychopath (also see Sociopath) An individual who has a specific personality disorder characterised by sometimes committing violent/antisocial acts, being deceitful, often with a failure to show guilt or remorse, exhibiting superficial charm, self-centred and can be incapable of love.

Pulse Rate Defined as the speed of the rhythm which is caused by the blood being forced through the arteries. 'Variability' often appended to indicate change in pulse rate.

Questions A word or sentence which is addressed to someone in order to gather information from their reply.

Reaction How an individual responds physically or emotionally to an action, conversation, situation or another stimulus.

Reflex A sometimes uncontrollable and often unconscious response to a stimulus.

Refractory Period	A period when an individual only filters in information that fits or supports the emotion or state that they are feeling.
Resonance	When one object vibrating at the same natural frequency of a second object forces that second object into vibrational motion. Now being applied to emotional contagion where the emotions of one person can create as similar emotion in others.
Response	Defined as a verbal, written and occasionally non-verbal answer.
Sad	An emotion described as the feeling of sorrow or unhappiness often brought on by the loss of a valued person or object.
Six Channel Analysis - Realtime	Or SCAnR. A comprehensive model which uses data from multi (communication) channels (Face/Body/Voice/Interaction Style/Verbal Content/Psychophysiology) and the use of real-time cognitive conversation to read, understand and influence others. Comprehensive system known as SCAnS (Six Channel Analysis System) – like FACS for all six channels.
Sclera	Defined as the white outer layer of the eyeball.

Script	A sequence of expected behaviours for a given situation – usually conditioned from powerful or early in life experiences. Silvan Tomkins recognized that our affective experiences fall into patterns that we may group together according to criteria such as the types of persons and places involved and the degree of intensity of the effect experienced.
Semantic	Relating to meaning, especially meaning of language.
Subtle Expression Training Tool	Or SETT. A type of facial expression recognition training tool created by Paul Ekman focusing on partial expressions.
Signals	Defined as an action, sound or gesture which is used in order to relay information or instructions to others.
Shrug	When an individual raises their shoulders or hands in an up and down or rotational action. Also the downward arching of the lips created by a chin thrust.
Sociopath	A person who has a personality disorder characterised by antisocial behaviour and who often lacks a sense of moral responsibility or social conscience.
Spontaneous	When something is done on a whim and without premeditation.

Startle Reflex A very quick unconscious physical reaction to a sudden stimulus.

Stimulus Something which causes a reaction within an organ or a tissue.

Stress Defined as a feeling of distress caused by the demand on an individual's physical or mental energy.

Surprise An emotional response to a trigger that is unexpected and sudden.

Statement Validity Assessment An analysis method used to establish the credibility of a statement put forward by an individual.

Taxonomy Defined as the classification of specific things e.g. facial expressions

Temperate Man A person who shows self-restraint and who does things in moderation.

Therapy Defined as a type of treatment which is used in order to try and alleviate various diseases or disorders, e.g. psychological.

Thermal Image A way of improving the visibility of people or objects when they are in darkness. This is done by detecting the infrared radiation which it emits which can then be used to create a proper image.

Trait Defined as a distinct characteristic found in a person.

Transference   The displacement of an emotion from one individual to another.

Trauma   A term used to describe either a psychological or physical injury.

Trigger   A stimulus that could be an event, relived or imagined which creates a response or reaction in a person.

Triune Brain   A model that describes the evolution of the vertebrate forebrain and behaviour. MacLean stated that the brain consisted of three complexes (reptilian, paleomammalian, neomamallian) which were added throughout evolution.

Truth Telling   A sincere attempt to provide accurate information.

Universal Facial Expression   Defined as facial expressions for the seven basic emotions which are innate and universal.

Verbal Communication   A form of communication which involves talking.

Verbal Content   Defined as what is included in a conversation between individuals.

Verbal Style   The way in which a person communicates with another person/persons.

Voice   A term referring to everything which is involved in the process of speech but not the words themselves. The sound produced by the vocal organs.

Voice Stress Analysis See 'Layered Voice Analysis'

Index

182

Endnotes

[1] https://www.eiagroup.com/about/the-team

[2] http://www.paulekman.com/paul-ekman

[3] https://en.wikipedia.org/wiki/Inside_Out_(2015_film)

[4] http://www.ekmaninternational.com

[5] His latest publication being 'Investigating Terrorism':

http://eu.wiley.com/WileyCDA/WileyTitle/productCd-1119994152.html

[6] http://www.leannetenbrinke.com

[7] http://stephenporter.org

[8] https://www.linkedin.com/in/mary-schollum-19910b29

[9] Especially work centered around this publication - Wright Whelan, C.,
Wagstaff, G.F. and Wheatcroft, J.M., 2014. High-stakes lies: Verbal and
nonverbal cues to deception in public appeals for help with missing or murdered
relatives. *Psychiatry, Psychology and Law*, *21*(4), pp.523-537.

[10] Archer, D.E. & Lansley, C.A. (2015). Public appeals, news interviews and
crocodile tears: an argument for multi-channel analysis. [Online] Available at:
http://www.euppublishing.com [Accessed 15 August 2015]. The Huntley clip
was also analysed by the author in the UK ITV documentary 'Lying Game –
Crimes that Fooled Britain' – see
https://www.youtube.com/watch?v=ySX7wMFbbzw&list=PL275AAE048584F22
9&index=17

[11] *Cognitive Load* is the total amount of mental effort being used in the working
memory.

[12] Porter & ten Brinke (2010) work extensively in this field and their research
supports our multi-channel approach and argue that,

> *"While the presence of a single behavioural cue may not provide convincing*
> *evidence for deception, the co-occurrence of multiple cues from words, body,*
> *and face should provide the lie catcher with increased confidence that*
> *deception has occurred. In situations that allow, the validity of such a multi-*
> *cue approach might be bolstered by the (comparable) baseline method. We*
> *suggest that if the lie catcher has the benefit of sound knowledge of a*

target's baseline truthful behaviour (ideally videotaped along with the potential deception) and observes a consistent change in illustrator use, pause length, speech rate and/or other behaviours, it may be evidence for deception to be considered along with other information. In an interview context, such behaviour should arouse suspicion and lead to focused questioning... while traditional deception research typically has focused on detection accuracy in 'passive' tasks such as judging videotaped speakers, recent work has been addressing the utility of 'strategic', active interviewing approaches."

Ref: Porter, S., & ten Brinke, L. (2010). The truth about lies: What works in detecting high-stakes deception? Invited article in a Special Issue of Legal and Criminological Psychology, 14, 119-134. doi:10.1348/135532509X433151

[13] Multichannel approaches are being used widely. See Matsumoto, D., Hwang, H.S., Skinner, L. and Frank, M., 2011. Evaluating truthfulness and detecting deception. *FBI law enforcement bulletin, 80,* pp.1-25 - https://leb.fbi.gov/2011/june/evaluating-truthfulness-and-detecting-deception. See also Pearse, J. and Lansley, C., 2010. Reading others. *Training Journal,* pp.62-5 - http://hdl.voced.edu.au/10707/52901.

[14] Ekman, P. (2009) Telling Lies : Clues to Deceit in the Marketplace, Politics, and Marriage. New York: Norton

[15] Zuckerman et al.'s (1981) four-factor theory: Zuckerman, M., DePaulo, B. M., & Rosenthal, R. (1981). Verbal and non-verbal communication of deception. In L. Berkowitz (Ed.), Advances in experimental social psychology (Vol. 14, pp. 1–59). New York: Academic Press.

[16] Paraphrased from longer definitions by Ekman, P., (2007). Emotions Revealed, Owl Books, 2nd Edition. Classic core book for understanding emotions.

[17] LeDoux, J., (1996). The Emotional Brain: The Mysterious Underpinnings of Emotional Life Published by Simon&Schuster.

[18] Ekman, P., (2007). Emotions Revealed, Owl Books, 2nd Edition.

[19] http://www.eiconsortium.org/ provides a good overview of some of the emotional intelligence models that have been developed.

[20] Ekman, P. (2001). Telling lies: Clues to deceit in the marketplace, politics, and marriage. New York: W W Norton & Co.. Actual quote from Othello is "Out, strumpet! weep'st thou for him to my face?".

[21] Archer, D.E. & Lansley, C.A. (2015). Public appeals, news interviews and crocodile tears: an argument for multi-channel analysis. [Online] Available at: http://www.euppublishing.com [Accessed 15 August 2015].

[22] 'Reading Others' article (Lansley and Pearse). First published in the Training Journal (2010) - http://www.ekmaninternational.com/media/4581/reading_others[2]%20cliff%20n%20john.pdf

[23] Pearse, J. and Lansley, C.A. (2010). 'Reading Others', Training Journal. October 2010, pp. 62–5. Available online at: http://j.mp/pearselansleyRO [Accessed 28 Aug 2015]

[24] LeDoux, J., (1996). The Emotional Brain: The Mysterious Underpinnings of Emotional Life Published by Simon&Schuster.

[25] LeDoux, J.E., 2008. Emotional colouration of consciousness: how feelings come about. Frontiers of consciousness: Chichele lectures, pp.69-130.

[26] Ekman, P., (2007). Emotions Revealed, Owl Books, 2nd Edition.

[27] https://en.wikipedia.org/wiki/Asperger_syndrome

[28] https://www.dropbox.com/s/df0do0ioucds3xp/Getting%20to%20the%20Truth%20-%20EIA%20White%20Paper%20Series%20312966-290815%20CAL.pdf?dl=0

[29] Archer, D.E. & Lansley, C.A. (2015). Public appeals, news interviews and crocodile tears: an argument for multi-channel analysis. [Online] Available at: http://www.euppublishing.com [Accessed 15 August 2015].

[30] See notes here on visual search https://en.wikipedia.org/wiki/Visual_search and on attention https://en.wikipedia.org/wiki/Attention and follow up links on automaticity and overt focus.

[31] http://www.emotional-intelligence-academy.com

[32] http://www.mindfulnesscds.com/

[33] Ranadivé, V. and Maney, K., 2011. The Two-Second Advantage: How We

Succeed by Anticipating the Future--Just Enough. Crown Business.

[34] I suggest you start with this book and then try his CDs: Kabat-Zinn, J., 2009. *Wherever you go, there you are: Mindfulness meditation in everyday life*. Hachette UK.

[35] What are the benefits of mindfulness. A wealth of new research has explored this age-old practice. Here's a look at its benefits for both clients and psychologists

http://www.apa.org/monitor/2012/07-08/ce-corner.aspx

[36] Porter, S., & ten Brinke, L. (2010). The truth about lies: What works in detecting high-stakes deception? Invited article in a Special Issue of Legal and Criminological Psychology, 14, 119-134. doi:10.1348/135532509X433151.

[37] Examples in other papers in these endnotes where abilities have jumped from around 50% to 80%+.

[38] Archer, D.E. & Lansley, C.A. (2015). Public appeals, news interviews and crocodile tears: an argument for multi-channel analysis. [Online] Available at: http://www.euppublishing.com [Accessed 15 August 2015].

[39] Huntley clip analysed by the author in the ITV documentary 'Lying Game – Crimes that Fooled Britain' – see

https://www.youtube.com/watch?v=ySX7wMFbbzw&list=PL275AAE048584F229&index=17

[40] Archer, D.E. & Lansley, C.A. (2015). Public appeals, news interviews and crocodile tears: an argument for multi-channel analysis. [Online] Available at: http://www.euppublishing.com [Accessed 15 August 2015].

[41] FACS = Facial Action Coding System – more information

https://en.wikipedia.org/wiki/Facial_Action_Coding_System

[42] Zuckerman et al.'s (1981) four-factor theory: Zuckerman, M., DePaulo, B. M., & Rosenthal, R. (1981). Verbal and non-verbal communication of deception. In L. Berkowitz (Ed.), Advances in experimental social psychology (Vol. 14, pp. 1–59). New York: Academic Press.

[43] https://en.wikipedia.org/wiki/Kato_Kaelin

[44] Here we used PRAAT software.

[45] https://www.washingtonpost.com/archive/lifestyle/1995/05/26/the-book-kato-kaelin-never-wrote/00b9c6e8-f968-4226-ac6c-5ec796f35a42/?utm_term=.fe96d5d1b6c3

[46] A higher-pitched voice has been suggested to be useful when seeking to identify potential deception in another. The idea - put forward by Ekman & Friesen (1976) amongst others – is that, as speakers deceive, they become psychologically and physiologically aroused in certain ways that tend to put stress/tension on vocal chords, leading to an increase in pitch. There are several reasons posited for this – the most popular being the notion that deception will be associated with a fear of getting caught – which can lead, in turn, to a would-be deceiver behaving nervously such that they use a higher-pitched voice (as well as more speech dis-fluencies) when conversing (Siegman, 1985). Care is needed again here due to the same effects from the fear of being disbelieved or anxiety about the test itself. A key thing to bear in mind is that, whilst some would-be deceivers might be nervous, we cannot assume that all those who engage in lying feel such fear (Vrij, 2008).

[47] Adapted from a similar grid by David Matsumoto: Matsumoto, D. and Frank, M.G., 2012. *Nonverbal Communication: Science and Applications: Science and Applications*. Sage.

[48] Picking up on voice quality and emotions and deception, some researchers have argued that this particular feature of our voice, as well as pitch, might present us with more clues than the words someone utters or their facial expressions, not least because – like body language – voice quality and vocal inflections are more difficult for a speaker to control. (DeLamater & Myers, 2010: 103)

[49] For more on this read - Pennebaker, J.W. 2011. The Secret Life of Pronouns: What our Words Say about us. New York, NY: Bloomsbury Press.

[50] The Philpotts' clip was analysed by the author in the UK ITV documentary 'Lying Game – Crimes that Fooled Britain' -

[51] This aspect of SCAnR may prove to be the most contentious, given CBCA was developed to assess witness credibility, not whether a person was telling the truth or being deceptive, and has previously struggled to distinguish short lies (non-experienced elements) within otherwise truthful stories (i.e., experienced events: see Vrij and Mann 2001). In our defence, we point to the fact we are not the only researchers to use CBCA in deception detection research (see, e.g., Vrij et al, 2004, 2007; Colwell, 2007), and the fact that our adapted version of CBCA is but one component of the SCAnR method.

[52] CBCA - Its purpose is to identify credibility characteristics – on the assumption that **accounts based on recollections of an actual event will differ quantitatively and qualitatively from fictitious accounts** (see Undeutsch, 1967). This assumption is commonly referred to as the Undeutsch Hypothesis. CBCA was designed with a specific text type in mind - that of children's narrative reports for the German Supreme Courts. These narratives, moreover, are meant to be as "pure" as possible. That is, the narrative has to be the children's own words – not primed in any way by questions they've been asked or any other third party influence. And the process itself is part of a much larger procedure which involves, first, a case-file analysis, followed, second, by an interview or interviews (which are then transcribed – before being coded for credibility criteria. And the occurrence – and, hence coding of these criteria isn't meant to point to truth. Rather, they point to the likelihood that that particular account is more credible because of the presence of specific credibility features. In SCAnR we have taken a bold step in reducing the 19 criteria down to seven and flipping them to be potential deception indicators and applying them to adults. This aspect of SCAnR may prove to be the most contentious to those in this field, given that CBCA was developed to assess witness credibility, not whether a person was telling the truth or being deceptive, and has previously struggled to distinguish short lies (non-experienced elements) within otherwise truthful stories (i.e., experienced events; see Vrij and Mann, 2001). In our defense, we point to the fact that we are not the only researchers to use CBCA in deception detection research (see, for example, Colwell, 2007; and Vrij et al., 2004, 2007), and the fact that our adapted version of CBCA is but one component, one Pin, of the SCAnR method.

[53] Archer, D.E. & Lansley, C.A. (2015). Public appeals, news interviews and crocodile tears: an argument for multi-channel analysis. [Online] Available at: http://www.euppublishing.com [Accessed 15 August 2015].

[54] The first experimental studies of memory were published in 1885 by German psychologist Hermann Ebbinghaus, and tens of thousands of memory studies have been conducted since (Loftus & Calvin, 2001). These clearly demonstrate that the human brain has the ability to retain a vast quantity of information and experience acquired over a lifetime. But memory is not like a video recorder that records everything it sees, or a computer that can retrieve everything stored on it. Instead:

"Human memory is cluttered. Memories don't get lost so much as they become distorted or hard to find. We may like to say that we've lost something - but often, an hour later, it pops uninvited into our consciousness, where it has been lurking all along. The serious difference between computer and human memory is that we don't pop out a pristine copy of the original event, the way a computer does. Instead, we reconstruct things as best we can from all the clutter. We guess. Often that isn't good enough, especially for a fair judicial process. Or just one's self respect; it's embarrassing to be badly wrong and we'll deny an error even to ourselves" (Loftus & Calvin, 2001). Sometimes we make mistakes. This is normal forgetting and should not be confused with deception.

[55] https://en.wikipedia.org/wiki/Personal-event_memory

[56] See our paper Archer, D.E. & Lansley, C.A. (2015). Other research has examined similar types of approach to determining truthfulness. For example, a recent FBI article outlines research in which 60 written suspect or victim statements taken during the investigation of violent crime and property crimes were analysed (Adams & Jarvis, 2004, pp7-12). Half the statements had been deemed by investigators to be truthful; the other half were deemed to be deceptive. Actual truthfulness or deception was determined through the conviction of the offender, overwhelming physical evidence, corroborated confession by the offender, or some combination of these. The researchers found a number of relationships between truthfulness and features of the examined statements. The Adams & Jarvis study (2004) is interesting for two reasons: 1) the focus is much more on helping investigators to find signs of truthfulness as opposed to the normal focus on deception; and 2) the

conclusions help to interpret responses to questions as well as written statements.

Deception

A great deal of detail about events leading up to the incident, but little critical information about the criminal incident in question. The suspect's or alleged victim's account of what happened is usually lacking in sensory details. Filled with vagueness and equivocation
(e.g., "someone" rather than "a tall man wearing a black ski mask"). An account of a created event is less likely to include affective information.

Features:

- The percentage of words in the part of the statement dealing with the criminal incident
- The inclusion of unique sensory details
- The inclusion of emotions (fear, anger, sadness, enjoyment, love, surprise, disgust and shame)

Truthfulness

The introductory part of the statement (which establishes the context of the crime) is much shorter than the criminal incident section (which says what happened, how it happened, where, who, when, etc). Truthful statements are much more likely to contain detailed depictions of the five senses (e.g., what they smelt, heard, tasted, felt (touched), or saw).
This is only significant in the criminal incident section of the statement as deceptive writers may include truthful sensory details in the introductory section. The concluding part of statements are likely to include emotional reactions (e.g., how scared they felt).
The research found this relationship was much stronger in statements about homicides than less serious crimes.

[57] In Sigmund Freud's 1901 book, *The Psychopathology of Everyday Life*.

[58] https://www.psychologytoday.com/articles/201203/slips-the-tongue - Jenna Pincott (March 13th, 2012)

[59] DePaulo, B. M., J.J. Lindsay, B.E., Malone, L. Muhlenbruck, K. Charlton, and H. Cooper. 2003. 'Cues to deception', *Psychological Bulletin* 129.

[60] Ekman, P. 2004. *Telling Lies: Clues to Deceit in the Marketplace, Politics and Marriage*. New York: W.W. Norton.

[61] http://www.paulekman.com/atlas-of-emotions/#more:annex-scientific-basis outlines this from the results of work done by Eve and Paul Ekman for the Atlas of Emotions initiative they completed with the Dalai Lama.

[62] https://en.wikipedia.org/wiki/Facial_Action_Coding_System

[63] Ten Brinke, L. and S. Porter. 2012. 'Cry me a river: Identifying the behavioural consequences of extremely high-stakes interpersonal deception'. *Law and Human Behaviour* 36 (6), pp. 469-77. Similar to ten Brinke and Porter (2012), we draw on insights from FACS-related research for the first of the five Face codes. Specifically, our (FACS-trained) SCAnR coders catalogue FACS anomalies via 18 of the key, emotion related, FACS codes.

[64] Ekman, P., (2007). Emotions Revealed, Owl Books, 2nd Edition.

[65] De Waal, F., 2007. *Chimpanzee politics: Power and sex among apes*. JHU Press.

[66] Credit: http://living-in-a-limited-world-to.blog.co.uk/2012/03/27/the-sullen-sulk-13315283/

[67] Ekman, P. and Friesen, W.V., 1982. Felt, false, and miserable smiles. *Journal of nonverbal behavior*, 6(4), pp.238-252.

[68] Sixteen Enjoyable Emotions article:
http://www.ekmaninternational.com/ResearchFiles/Sixteen-Enjoyable-Emotions-Paul-Ekman.pdf

[69] See http://www.scholarpedia.org/article/Facial_expression_analysis and also Matsumoto, D. and Lee, M., 1993. Consciousness, volition, and the neuropsychology of facial expressions of emotion. *Consciousness and Cognition*, 2(3), pp.237-254.

[70] Three papers here –

1. Ekman, P. (2003). Darwin, Deception, and Facial Expression, *Annals of New York Academy of Sciences*, 1000: 205–221

2. EKMAN, P. & W.V. FRIESEN. 1982. Felt, false and miserable smiles. J. Nonverb. Behav. 6: 238–252.

3. Ekman, P., and M. Frank. 1993. *Not all Smiles are Created Equal: The Differences between Enjoyment and Non-Enjoyment Smiles.* San Francisco: University of California.

N.B. Ekman(2003) argues in this paper(above) that, "the bulk of the findings I have described in this chapter pertain to smiling, my expectation that findings apply to other emotional expressions has been supported by those studies that have examined other expressions".

http://www.mapageweb.umontreal.ca/tuitekj/cours/2611pdf/ekman-darwin.pdf

[71] Ekman, P. (2003). Darwin, Deception, and Facial Expression, *Annals of New York Academy of Sciences*, 1000: 205–221

[72] Hess, U. and Kleck, R.E., 1990. Differentiating emotion elicited and deliberate emotional facial expressions. *European Journal of Social Psychology*, 20(5), pp.369-385. See also Frank, M.G. and Ekman, P., 1993. Not all smiles are created equal: The differences between enjoyment and nonenjoyment smiles. *Humor-International Journal of Humor Research*, 6(1), pp.9-26.

[73] LEAL, S. and VRIJ, A., 2008. Blinking during and after lying. Journal of Nonverbal Behaviour, 32(4), pp. 187-194.

[74] Hartwig and Bond, 2011; Vrij and Granhag, 2012.

[75] This model is adapted from a framework originated in 2010 by Dr John Pearse and Cliff Lansley in training courses designed with Dr Paul Ekman (www.paulekman.com) and Emotional Intelligence Academy (www.EIAGroup.com) for *Paul Ekman International*. It also features in the *Encyclopedia of Forensic and Legal Medicine*.

[76] See Daniel Schacter's 'Seven Sins of Memory' in this book

https://www.amazon.co.uk/Seven-Sins-Memory-Forgets-Remembers/dp/0618219196 or a synopsis here

https://en.wikipedia.org/wiki/The_Seven_Sins_of_Memory

Lightning Source UK Ltd.
Milton Keynes UK
UKOW07f0006150517
301148UK00013B/80/P